T0072513

THE
REDEMPTION
LETTERS

FROM DEATH ROW TO HEAVEN:
An Account of Salvation from the Darkest of Places

LeAnn Ploeger

WESTBOW
PRESS®
A DIVISION OF THOMAS NELSON
& ZONDERVAN

WestBow Press books may be ordered through booksellers or by contacting:

WestBow Press
A Division of Thomas Nelson & Zondervan
1663 Liberty Drive
Bloomington, IN 47403
www.westbowpress.com
844-714-3454

Interior Image Credit: Edward Frias

ISBN: 978-1-6642-6301-7 (sc)
ISBN: 978-1-6642-6302-4 (hc)
ISBN: 978-1-6642-6303-1 (e)

Library of Congress Control Number: 2022906303

Print information available on the last page.

WestBow Press rev. date: 5/12/2022

For my momma

INTRODUCTION

The following letters are very personal to me, not to mention very private. Until I decided to write this book, no one other than me had ever read them. My family knew about them, of course, maybe a couple of my friends, but otherwise they were of a confidential matter.

I was a teenage girl screaming in my skin. I had anxiety coupled with depression, a mild eating disorder, and low self-esteem. I lacked a permanent female figure in my life, and my father was an alcoholic who had no idea how to raise a teenage girl. I was desperate for someone to talk and connect with. I needed someone who wouldn't judge me for my rage, my outburst, my oftentimes violent temper.

I found that connection with my correspondence to Roger Dale. He didn't judge; he related. He didn't mock me; he understood and identified. He listened to my drama, complaints, and lack of understanding life due to my young age all the while praying for me and witnessing about our Lord Jesus. He reinforced that I am loved, I am worthy, and I have an adoring Heavenly Father who created me with a purpose—for a purpose!

Our God started this journey with Roger Dale and me before I even knew who he was, before I ever wrote any letters. Jesus knew at this certain point in my life I would need a friend who was constant, unconventional, and perhaps one who needed my friendship as much as I needed his.

So, as you read these letters, be open-minded and openhearted, and let the words of a redeemed man speak to you as they spoke to me.

PREFACE

The carpet was scratchy on my belly as I sprawled out in front of the TV. The ABC nightly news report was on and we (my brothers, father, and I) were engaged with the day's happenings. The reporter finished one story and then quickly started another. He was discussing a twenty-seven-year anniversary about a group of murders. The hostility culled with sadness in his tone kept my attention. Who was this man he was speaking of? Who was Charles Manson, and what did he do that was so terrible that it was being covered on national television?

"Dad, what are they talking about? Who is that guy?" I asked. My father peeked over his crossword puzzle from the couch. "Just some guy that killed a bunch of people," he replied. Then he motioned for me to turn back around to listen.

After announcing Manson's parole was denied, the reporter started telling of a book. *Helter Skelter* was written about the murders and trial. A whole book written about this guy? My curiosity was growing. By the time the news story ended, I had already stopped listening. My thoughts were left with the Manson murders. I wanted to find out what really happened and who this person was.

Searching the bookstore, I found the criminal history section, and sure enough, there it was. Its black cover with red lettering was glaring back at me: Helter Skelter, written by prosecuting attorney Vincent Bugliosi, offered such explicit detail to the crime I ended up reading the book twice and was fascinated by what I learned. One man did all that? How is that possible?

I was determined to find out. I discovered in the afterward of the book where Manson was housed. A trip to the local post office yielded the zip code. With my newly discovered information, I was ready to begin my letter.

A few weeks went by after I wrote to Charlie. No response. So I wrote him again. No response. One more try? No response. OK, last shot and then I'd be done. No response.

Then one cold day in December 1996, I received a letter! My father was furious when he handed me the post. *"What have you been doing?"* he screamed.

I took the letter and ran up to my room, hands trembling. I opened the pale-yellow envelope with the red label reading, "California State Prison Corcoran," in upper right corner.

```
LeAnn: My name is Roger Dale Smith.
I'm writing to you in regards to the
four letters you've sent Charlie ...
```

Wow! I got a response! Someone wrote me back! But who is Roger Dale? Why is he writing me and not Charlie?

Buy the next morning, the reality of what I had possession of was evident. This letter was from Charles Manson's best friend and cellmate, and he was writing me!

I must respond and learn more. But little did I know that a simple letter written out of curiosity to one person would lead to a great friendship with another. Those beginning letters of correspondence turned into a close, personal friendship with a man whose newfound relationship with Jesus would guide me through some of the hardest times of my young life.

Roger Dale Smith became my best friend and confidant, a mentor who grew to love me as a daughter. He had lived his life lost and condemned but found his salvation with Jesus Christ in the darkest of places.

These following letters are some of the times we shared. His love for Jesus can be felt strongly as he talks about his past sins, knowing they have *all* been forgiven and that even someone like him can go to heaven having been forgiven by the redeeming blood of Jesus Christ! Roger Dale lived with the full understanding that no sin is unforgiveable and that the blood of Jesus washed him clean!

These letters are his testimony.

LETTER 1

Roger Dale Smith
A-43198-C   4A-4R-47-L
Corcoran State Prison
Corcoran, California
                    93212

CALIFORNIA
STATE PRISON
CORCORAN

U.S. POSTAGE
$0.32

Photo Enclosed!

Ms. Le Ann Redding
P.O. Box # ███
Sardis, Tennessee
                    38371

11/28/96
Thanksgiving Day

LeAnn:

My name is Roger Dale Smith. I'm writing to you in regards to the four letters you've sent Charlie and your poem "When We Come Around." I'm also writing you because you seem like a nice person and I believe you need to know why you haven't received a reply to your letter until now. Please bear with me as I try to explain.

I was on "Death Row" when Charlie came there in 1971. He was my neighbor in the cell next to mine and, over time, we became pretty good friends. That friendship has only gotten stronger over the years.

As you can imagine, <u>back then</u>, Charlie was on the cover of nearly every magazine and newspaper in the <u>world</u>! Not just this country-but the entire world. And the so-called "press"-written and electronic-made him out to be a "devil", a "madman", a "mass murderer." All that negative stuff.

LeAnn, Charlie Manson never killed anyone! <u>Never</u>! The rest of us up there on the "Row" were guilty of murder including me. Charlie was not. That was what made Charlie "unique" to me.

Anyway, Charlie received <u>thousands</u> of letters and cards from people all over the world. LeAnn, Charlie couldn't even read and write! When the guards brought the mail, they would bring (30) or (40) letters for the rest of us-and hundreds of letters & cards addressed to Charlie! And here he is, can't even read or write! Anyway, Charlie would give me all these hundreds of letters <u>every day</u> and I'd go through them looking for certain names, "family members" which I'd then read to Charlie and then answer for him. He very seldom even wanted to hear any of the other letters. Out of curiosity mostly, I'd read all of them and, every once in a while, I'd answer a letter that I thought deserved a reply.

Well, this went on for a long time while we were on the "Row" and even after we got off the "Row." That was a long time ago. Anyway, Charlie learned to read & write. Now, when he receives a letter from a "family member," he can and does read & write them back. But LeAnn, even though he doesn't get hundreds of letters each day anymore, he still gets a <u>lot</u> of mail!! Far more than he can answer.

Look girl, I was born in Brownsville, Tennessee! I was raised in Ripley, Jackson, Milan, Lexington, and Trenton, Tennessee. Even though I've been out here in California, <u>in prison</u>, for almost (40) years, I'm still an old Tennessee boy at heart! And truthfully, <u>that</u> is the real reason I'm writing this letter to <u>you</u>! You are my "Home Girl" and I simply had to write and tell you what is going on. When someone takes the time & effort to write a nice letter, <u>to me</u>, they deserve a reply. It's that simple to me.

But, to Charlie, he receives hundreds of letters from hundreds of strangers! How can he, even if wanted to, answer all of these letters? And, how many people do you think even take the time to enclose a book of stamps—or even one stamp! Very, very few. And, even if he wanted to do so, which he doesn't, could he answer all these letters and cards he receives! There is just no way. And, with each costing 32 cents, every (2) letters would be out of his pocket! In a few months he would go just on postage alone! Hah!

Anyway, your letters made me take notice. you seem like a nice kid and you are state. Plus, I liked your poem! Smile! (
by the way!)

For these reasons I'm writing you this letter and I'm enclosing a picture of Charlie & I which we took a couple of weeks ago. Hope you like it.

Okay, LeAnn, I guess that's about all I got to say. You take care of yourself. By the way, "LeAnn" is a beautiful name!! (Smile!)

Take Care "Featherwood",
Roger Dale

11/28/96

Thanksgiving Day

Le Ann:

My name is ~~Roger~~ Dale Smith. I'm writing to you in regards to the four letters you've sent Charlie and your poem, "When We Come Around". I'm also writing you because you seem like a nice person and I believe you need to know why you haven't received a reply to your letters until now. Please bear with me as I try to explain.

I was on "Death Row" when Charlie came there in 1971. He was my neighbor in the cell next to mine and, over time, we became pretty good friends. That friendship has only gotten stronger over the years.

As you can imagine, ~~back then~~, Charlie was on the cover of nearly every magazine and newspaper in the ~~world~~! Not just this country — but the ~~entire~~ world. And the so-called "press" — written and electronic — made him out to be a "devil", a "madman", a "mass murderer". All that negative ▮▮▮.

Le Ann, Charlie Manson never killed anyone! Never! The rest of us up there on the "Row" were guilty of murder including me. Charlie was not. That was what made Charlie "unique" to me.

Anyway, Charlie received ~~thousands~~ of letters and cards from people all over the world. Le Ann, Charlie couldn't even read and write! When the guards brought the mail, they would bring (30) or (40) letters for the rest of us — and hundreds of letters & cards addressed to Charlie! And here he is, can't even read or write! Anyway, Charlie would give me all these hundreds of letters every day and I'd go through them looking for certain names, "family members", which I'd then read to Charlie and then answer for him. He very seldom even wanted to hear any of the other letters. Out of curiosity mostly, I'd read all of them and, every once in awhile, I'd answer a letter that I thought deserved a reply.

Well, this went on for a long time while we were on the "Row" and even after we got off the "Row". That was a long time ago. Anyway, Charlie learned to read & write. Now, when he receives a letter from a "family member", he can and does read & write them back. But Le Ann, even though he doesn't get hundreds of letters each day anymore, he still gets a lot of mail! Far more than he can answer.

Look girl, I was born in Brownsville, Tennessee! I was raised in Ripley, Jackson, Milan, Lexington and Trenton, Tennessee. Even though I've been out here in California, in prison, for almost (40) years, I'm still an old Tennessee boy at heart! And truthfully, that is the real reason I'm writing this letter to you! You are my "Home Girl" and I simply had to write and tell you what is going on. When someone takes the time & effort to write a nice letter, to me, they deserve a reply. It's that simple to me.

— 3 —

But, to Charlie, he receives hundreds of letters from hundreds of strangers! How can he, even if he wanted to, answer all of these letters? And, how many people do you think even take the time to enclose a book of stamps — or even one stamp? Very, very few. So, even if he wanted to do so, which he doesn't, how could he answer all these letters and cards he still receives? There is just no way. And, with each stamp costing 32¢, every (3) letters would be a dollar out of his pocket! ████, in a few months he would be broke just on postage alone! hah!

Anyway, your letters made me take notice because you seem like a nice kid and you are from my home state. Plus, I liked your poem! Smile! (So did Charlie by the way!)

For these reasons I'm writing you this letter and I'm enclosing a picture of Charlie & I which we took a couple of weeks ago. Hope you like it.

Okay Le Ann, I guess that's about all I got to say. You take care of yourself. By the way, "Le Ann" is a beautiful name! (Smile!)

Take Care "Featherwood",

Roger Dale ✳:

11/9/96 To LeAnn
Tennessee Girl!!

WHEN WE COME AROUND

When we come around,
Hell's heat chasten
Full of shame and guilt,
Up at night pacin',
Our heart full of regret,
our soul full of remorse.
Along life's narrow way
And evil-laden course,
Grace favors death
With open arms strong.
Escape to survive;
Try to move along.
When we come around;
time life's sand
Evil is grasped,
Trapped by the walking man.
White turns to black;
With poisoned minds,
Helter Skelter is everywhere,
Painted among the signs.
A rise need to start;
The world is coming down
Maybe someday we'll understand
When we come around.

                            - LeAnn Redding

MEMORANDUM
OF CALL

Previous editions usable

TO:

☐ YOU WERE CALLED BY –   ☐ YOU WERE VISITED BY –

OF (Organization)

☐ PLEASE PHONE ▶   ☐ FTS   ☐ AUTOVON

☐ WILL CALL AGAIN   ☐ IS WAITING TO SEE YOU

☐ RETURNED YOUR CALL   ☐ WISHES AN APPOINTMENT

MESSAGE

*Corcoran CA
93212*

RECEIVED BY	DATE	TIME

63-110   NSN 7540-00-634-4018   STANDARD FORM 63 (Rev. 8-81)
Prescribed by GSA
☆ U.S.G.P.O. : 1993 342-198/80009   FPMR (41 CFR) 101—11.6

Very truly I tell you, the one who believes has eternal life

(John 6:47 NIV)

In God's mercy and grace, He forgives us and still loves us despite ourselves.

(Jeanette Duby)

LETTER 2

Roger Dale Smith
A-93198-C   4A-4R-47-L
Corcoran State Prison
Corcoran, California
                    93212

STATE
PRISON
CORCORAN

Ms. Le Ann Redding
P.O. Box #█
Sardis, Tennessee
                    38371

Hello "Featherwood"!

I received your letter, and poem, dated 12/6/96- but postmarked 12/24/96 at Lexington, Tennessee. So from the day you wrote the letter on 12/6/96, it took you (18) days to get it in the mail! Why? I'm really just curious so I thought I'd ask.

Your letter arrived here on 1/9/97 but I didn't get it until last night 1/13/97. All of this information comes from the envelope which I'm enclosing so you can actually see all the dates.

Check this out! You must be very close to where all my people live!! My momma, a sister and (2) brothers live in Lexington, Tenn!! Another (2) brothers and (1) sister live in Cedar Grove, Tenn which is only a few miles from Lexington! Also, I have aunts & uncles in Lexington, Hundington, Trenton and Milan, Tennessee. Plus Jackson, Ripton, Memphis, Foelton, & Jordonia, Tennessee. No kidding girl, I got <u>big family</u> back there!! And the hub of all the family is Lexington!! For them to postmark your letter in Lexington has got to mean that you live pretty close to there, doesn't it?

And I can relate to living back in the "woods"!! (Smile!) So did I when I was a kid in Cedar Grove. I was pretty much raised, until age (6) with my grandparents and we lived way, way back in the woods. We had no TV but we never missed it a bit. We had too much fun fishing, hunting, and raising dogs & chickens!

LeAnn, my family were and still are "poor people." We used to go into Lexington town once a month to pick-up "governments". (Federal food programs that distribute flour, cheese, peanut butter, and molasses.) That was the only time we "went to town" and it was a big event. The rest of the time, it was all about the "woods".

So, yes, a lot of what you write about is very, very special to me. We also went (muddin') & raced old cars & trucks on the back roads. Girl, do I miss being back there!! Whew! I'm a "Tennessee Boy" to the bone!! No, I don't know where Scotts Hill is but, once again, I'm assuming it's pretty close to Lexington isn't it?

Lynard Skynard is cool. Because I'm older I prefer a lot of country "oldies". I'm more into Hank Williams, Hank Snow, Lefty Frizzel, Patsy Cline, Lorretta Lynn, Conway Twitty, George Jones and Tammy Wynette. But, <u>if</u> I had to pick just (<u>1</u>) person whom personifies what I think county music should be about, it would be Merle Haggard. I'm telling you girl, that ole boy has got it all together in his music. <u>Everything</u>!!

Listen, LeAnn, don't ever let anyone tell you not to write or that your "insane" for writing. Writing is a form of expression which is very self-satisfying in many unique ways. Poetry is the heart & soul of mankind. It is a way to express feelings & thoughts that might otherwise be pent up inside and lead to all kinds of psychiatric problems. So, express yourself via your poetry and you'll never be "insane".

I'd be proud to be your pen-pal and, in time, your friend. If there is <u>anything</u> you want to ask me, don't hesitate. Please! If I can answer your questions, I'll do so. If I can't, I'll simply tell you I can't. Okay? Okay!!

Okay "Featherwood", it's time for me to sign-off and get some Z's. You be cool and write whenever you feel the need to share some of your thoughts. Oh yeah! there is just no way you can convince me you don't have any pictures of yourself and family!! Come on now!! But, it ain't no big thing. When & if you want to send me some flicks-do so!! Until then, I'll simply think of you as my little "Tennessee Featherwood"!! (Smile!)

Take Care!
Roger Dale

1/14/97

Hello "Featherwood"!

I received your letter, and poem, dated 12/6/96 — but postmarked 12/24/96 at Lexington, Tennessee. So, from the day you wrote the letter on 12/6/96, it took you (18) days to get it in the mail! Why? I'm really just curious so I thought I'd ask.

Your letter arrived here on 1/9/97 but I didn't get it until last night 1/13/97. All of this information comes from the envelope which I'm enclosing so you can actually see all the dates.

Check this out! You must be very close to where all my people live! My moma, a sister and (2) brothers live in Lexington, Tenn.! Another (2) brothers and (1) sister live in Cedar Grove, Tenn. which is only a few miles from Lexington! Also, I have aunts & uncles in Lexington, Huntington, Trenton and Milan, Tennessee. Plus Jackson, Ripton, Memphis, Felton & Jordonia, Tennessee. No ███████ girl, I got big family back there! And the hub of all the family is Lexington. For them to postmark your letter in Lexington has got to mean that you live pretty close to there, doesn't it?

And I can relate to living back in the "woods"! (Smile!) So did I when I was a kid in

Cedar Grove. I was pretty much raised, until age (6), with my grandparents and we lived way, way back in the woods. We had no TV but we never missed it a bit. We had too much fun fishing, hunting and raising dogs & chickens!

Le Ann, my family were and still are "poor people". We used to go into Lexington town once a month to pick-up "governments". (Federal food programs that distribute flour, cheese, peanut butter and molasses.) That was the only time we "went to town" and it was a big event. The rest of the time, it was all about the "woods".

So, yes, a lot of what you write about is very, very special to me. We also went (muddin') & raced old cars & trucks on the back roads. Still, do I miss being back there!! Whew! I'm a "Tennessee Boy" to the bone!! No, I don't know where Scott's Hill is but, once again, I'm assuming it's pretty close to Lexington isn't it?

Lynard Skynard is cool. Because I'm older I prefer a lot of country "oldies". I'm more into Hank Williams, Hank Snow, Lefty Frizzel, Patsy Cline, Loretta Lynn, Conway Twitty, George Jones and Tammy Wynette. But, if I had to pick just (1) person whom personifies what I think country music should be about, it would be Merle Haggard. I'm telling you girl, that ole boy has got it all together in his music. Everything!!

Listen LeAnn, don't ever let anyone tell you not to write or that your "████" for writing. Writing is a form of expression which is very self-satisfying in many unique ways. Poetry is the heart & soul of mankind. It is a way to express feelings & thoughts that might otherwise be pent up inside and lead to all kinds of psychiatric problems. So, express yourself via your poetry and you'll never be "████".

I'd be proud to be your pen-pal and, in time, your friend. If there is anything you want to ask me, don't hesitate. Please! If I can answer your questions, I'll do so. If I can't, I'll simply tell you I can't. Okay? Okay!!

Okay "Featherwood", it's time for me to sign-off and get some Z's. You be cool and write whenever you feel the need to share some of your thoughts. Oh yeah! there is just no way you can convince me you don't have any pictures of yourself and family!! Come on now!! But, it ain't no big thing. When & if you want to send me some flicks do so!! Until then, I'll simply think of you as my little "Tennessee Featherwood" (Smile)

Take Care!

Roger Dale

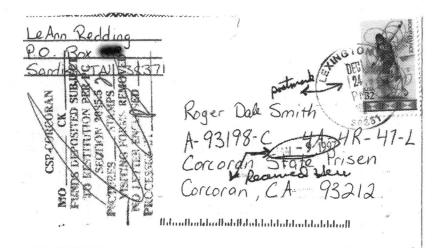

LeAnn Redding
P.O. Box ████
Sardi██ UTAH 3837I

CSP-CORCORAN
CK
FUNDS DEPOSITED SUBJECT
TO RESTITUTION PER
SECTION 2085.5
PICTURES
STAMPS
NOTES
NO LETTER ENCLOSED
RETURNING FUNDS REMOVED
M/O
PROCESSED

postmark →

Roger Dale Smith
A-93198-C   4A HR-47-L
Corcoran State Prisen
Corcoran, CA   93212

LEXINGTON
DEC 24
PM 82

received here

Peter replied, "Repent and be baptized, every one of you, in the name of Jesus Christ for the forgiveness of your sins. And you will receive the gift of the Holy Spirit."

(Acts 2:38 NIV)

When you make a mistake and the devil comes and tells you, "You're no good," you don't have to take on the guilt and condemnation he wants to put on you. No! You can immediately confess your mistake to God, thank Him for forgiving you and cleansing you with the blood of Jesus, and move forward in the victory of His grace and forgiveness.

(Joyce Meyer)

LETTER 3

Roger Dale Smith
A-43198-C   4A-4R-57-L
Corcoran State Prison
Corcoran, California
              93212

STATE
PRISON
CORCORAN

Le Ann Redding
P.O. Box # ▉
Sardis, Tennessee
                    38371

3/2/97

"Featherwood"

Hello "Tennessee Girl"!! I just got your letter and the picture this past week! I was glad to hear from you! And, I'm glad you sent me a picture. It kind of helps to have a picture whenever you write someone. It gives you an idea of what kind of person they are just by different things you see in the picture. Thank you for the picture, LeAnn!!

Hey! I told you I'd answer any question you might want to ask. It's only natural to want to get to know someone you don't know-and the only way to find out the things you may want to know is to ask. So, please, LeAnn, feel free to ask anything you may want to know. I'll answer anything you ask if I can, okay? Okay!!

As for my people, let me tell you all that I can. My grandmother was named M***. She was from Cedar Grove, Tennessee. She had several children. There was J***, J***, L***, L***, B*** and my mother L***. My mother, who goes by the name "K***" married my dad, J****, in Ripton, Tennessee in 1947. I am the first of (6) children. I was born on 4/24/47 in Brownsville, Tennessee. My mom was only (13) when she got pregnant with me and I was born when she was only (14) years old. I don't know many of my father's people.

I know he had C***, L***, V***, and C**** as his brothers & sisters. My aunts "T**" & L*** are now dead. My aunt V**** lives in Virginia and my uncle C**** lives in Las Vegas, Nevada. My dad was killed in a car crash in Peru, Indiana in 1967. I never really knew him. My uncles, J**** and J**** both died in Lexington, Tennessee. My aunt L*** and my aunt L*** married two brothers, F** & G**** and I think they both live in Huntingdon, Tenn. So does my little brother T**. My mom now lives in Huntingdon, Tenn. My brothers, R**** & J**** and M**** live in Lexington, Tenn. & Florida. My dad married another woman and I have (2) more brothers, J**** & T**** whom live in Lexington with their mom L***. I also have (2) other sisters, G**** in Buffalo, New York and B**** in Naples, Florida.

Shortly after I was born, my mom was simply too young to really care for me so she took me to her mother to raise. She did the same with R****, J*** and K****. My grandmother married S**** and I was raised by my grandma & grandpa until I was (6) years old, R**** was (4 1/2), J**** was (3) and K**** was just a little baby a few months old. At that time, in about 1954, we were living with my maternal grandparents in Milan, Tennessee, when my mom met & married W****.

Well they came and got us (4) kids and we moved to Klamath Falls, Oregon, which is where his people lived. My mom swears my daddy was a drunk and he beat her pretty bad. I don't know if that was true or not. Anyway, in Klamath Falls, Oregon, W**** people were really good people. They treated us pretty good but, W**** was one sick, sorry man! He got off on beating us kids pretty bad. Not "spankings" or even "whippings"- this guy really beat us BAD!! Being the eldest, I caught it the worse.

Anyway, in 1957, while beating us with a rubber shower hose with a big metal head on it, he hit my little brother J**** right in the forehead and it cut him to the bone. They had to call an ambulance and the hospital called the law! Well, when they took us (3) boys down to the police station and talked with us, they stripped us naked and took some pictures of us with all kinds of bruises all over our bodies. Those cops just got real mad!! They put W**** in jail that same night and took us (3) boys to juvenile hall.

Well, W**** people had money and they got him off

with no prison time. My two brothers went back with him & my mom but they didn't want me there no more. That was fine with me because I hated that man!! I hated and feared him BAD!!

So, here I was, (10) years old and no place to go. I went to several foster homes in the next (2) years. None of them seemed to work but for different reasons. Finally, I was sent to the "Corvallis Farm Home for Unwanted Children" in Corvallis, Oregon. I never forgot that one word: "Unwanted." I stayed there about a year and me and another boy (14) years old he was, ran off and broke into a bunch of houses and tried to steal a couple of cars.

For this, I was sent to "McClaren School for Boys" at Woodburn, Oregon. This was a real "reformatory" and I was there for (18) months. I learned how to fight, smoke, cuss, and all about girls there at "Woodburn."

In the meantime, my mom finally got tired of W**** and she moved back to Jackson, Tenn., with her mom and took my (2) brothers & baby sister with her. When I got paroled out of Woodburn in 1960, I was almost (13) years old and I was a little juvenile delinquent. They paroled me back to Tennessee in the care of my mom.

Needless to say, I just couldn't re-adjust to the "free world". I was no longer happy just being a little ignorant Tennessee "hillbilly". I was a little delinquent and in less than (6) months- we had moved to Lexington, Tennessee, where my mom started living with a man named R****. He was the sheriff of that county!! (Later on.)

Anyway, pretty soon I got caught stealing and me and another guy, G****, got sent to the "State Vocational School for White Boys" at Jordonia, Tennessee. I was there for a year, got out and was back in jail within a month! (Smile!) This time I was sent to the "Tennessee Youth Center" at Joelton, Tennessee and I was there for (1 1/2) years. I joined the U.S. Marine Corps and went to Parris Island, South Carolina for boot camp, then to Camp LaJune, North Carolina for A.I.T and then to Cherry Point, North Carolina, where I was stationed.

In Feb. of 1965 me and another Marine went A.W.O.L. and went to his home in Shellyville, Indiana. We pulled an armed robbery and got caught. We got kicked out of the Marine Corps and got a (2) years to (10) years sentence at the "Indiana State Penal Farm" at Greencastle, Indiana. I was there (4) months and escaped.

I went all over Indiana, Ohio, Missouri, Tennessee, Florida, Mississippi, Mexico, and finally here in Stockton, California. I robbed stores, gas stations, banks, department stores and stole all kinds of cars. Finally, on June 7, 1965, in Stockton, California, while drinking with a car full of girls & boys, all of us (17) & (18) years old, we get pulled over by Johnny Law and all my robbing & stealing caught up with me. I got sent to prison for (20) years.

But, when I got to prison, all the prison "gang wars" were going on. The Blacks had the "Black Guerilla Family" (B.G.F.) the Mexicans had the "Mexican Mafia" (EME) and the "Nuestra Familia" (N.F.) and we whites had a group called the "Aryan Brotherhood" (A.B.)

Because I was (18) years old, born in Tennessee, ex-Marine and has some "heart" I was soon caught-up in the middle of some, excuse my French, "serious stuff." Between 1965 and 1967 I was involved in several stabbings and five killings. By the time I was (21) years old, I was on "Death Row" condemned to die for (2) prison murders. I actually grew-up on "Death Row." I was up there for (7 1/2) years waiting to be executed. That's where I met Charlie.

Anyway, the death penalty was abolished in 1974 and

I came off the "Row" with a death sentence commuted to "life imprisonment without the possibility of parole". I've been doing that sentence all these years. I've served over (40) years locked-up in my (49) years on this earth. I've done over (32) years solid without having been out for even (1) single day!

LeAnn, I take no pride in what I've done with my life. I've never hurt a woman or a child-nor would I. It's just not in me. But, I have done some serious wrong in my life and I'm paying for it. I'm not "sniveling" or "whining". I did the crimes and now I'm doing the time. But, you did ask and now you know. I'm not a very "nice guy" at all!!

I will say one thing in my behalf. I did all this wrong when I was a young stupid kid trying to be a "tough guy". I've committed no kind of serious crime since Nov. 6, 1969, when I killed another "tough guy" in a knife fight where he was doing his best to kill me. So, for the past (28) years I've done no violence to anyone other than a fist-fight every now & then. Still, I did what I did and I continue to pay for what I did.

Look, "Featherwood", my people raised me up in the Pentecostal faith. Though I don't live like I should, I will tell you that I believe in the Lord Jesus Christ and I pray to God that I'll be forgiven for my sins and that I'll not go to hell. I can only hope that God will see fit to grant me eternal life in a place far better than this place has been for me. Amen!!

Okay, this has been a tough letter to write. A lot of bad memories. I've tried not to make excuses for what I've done and I've been honest with you because you wanted to know. It's not very pretty, is it? No, I can't say I'm very proud of what I've done. I can say that I'm sorry for much of what I've done, not all of it, and that I'd like to make whatever amends I can with what time I've got left.

Listen, LeAnn, <u>you</u> bring a little sunlight into a pretty dark place. Take care and write whenever you wish. I am here and I am …

Your Friend, Roger Dale

"Featherwood"   3/2/97

          Hello "Tennessee Girl"!! I just got your
letter and the picture this past week! I was glad to hear from
you! And, I'm glad you sent me a picture. It kind of helps
to have a picture whenever you write someone. It gives you an
idea of what kind of person they are just by different things
you see in the picture. Thank you for the picture Je Ann".
          Hey! I told you I'd answer any question
you might want to ask. It's only natural to want to get
to know someone you don't know — and the only way to find
out the things you may want to know is to ask. So, please,
Je Ann, feel free to ask anything you may want to know.
I'll answer anything you ask if I can, okay? Okay".
          As for my people, let me tell you all
that I can. My grandmother was named ███████
████████. She was from Cedar Grove, Tennessee.
She had several children. There was ███████████
██████, ███████████, ███████, ████████████ and
my mother ████████████. My mother, who goes by
the name "████" married my dad, ███████████
████████, in Ripton, Tennessee in 1947. I am the first
of (6) children. I was born on 4/24/47 in Brownsville
Tennessee. My mom was only (13) when she got pregnant
with me and I was born when she was only (14) years
old. I don't know many of my father's people.
                                        (OVER)

I know he had ███████, ███, ████ and █████████ as his brothers & sisters. My aunts "████" & ███ are now dead. My aunt ██████ lives in Virginia and my uncle ████████ lives in Las Vegas, Nevada. My dad was killed in a car crash in Peru, Indiana in 1967. I never really knew him. My uncles, ████████████ and ███████████ both died in Lexington, Tennessee. My aunt ██████ and my aunt ██████ married two bro- thers, ████████ & ████████████ and I think they both live in Huntingdon, Tenn. My sister, ████████ ███████, lives there in Lexington, Tenn. So does my little brother ██████. My mom now lives in Huntingdon, Tenn. My brothers, █████████████████████ & and ███████████████████ live in Lexington, Tenn. & Florida. My dad married another woman and I have (3) more brothers, ██████████████ & ████████████ whom live in Lexington with their mom ████. I also have (2) other sisters, ████████ in Buffalo, New York and ████ ██████ in Naples, Florida.

Shortly after I was born, my mom was sim- ply too young to really care for me so she took me to her mother to raise. She did the same with ███████, ██████ and ████████. My grandmother married █████████ and I was raised by my grandma & grandpa until I was (6) years old, ██████ was (4½), ██████ was (3) and ████████ was just a little baby a few months old.

At that time, in about 1954, we were living with my maternal grandparents in Milan, Tennessee, when my mom met & married █████████.

Well, they came and got us (4) kids and we moved to Klamath Falls, Oregon; which is where his people lived. My mom swears my daddy was a drunk and he beat her pretty bad. I don't know if that was true or not. Anyway, in Klamath Falls, Oregon, ██████ people were ████ good people. They treated us pretty good but, ████████████ was one sick, sorry S.O.B.! He got off on beating us kids pretty bad. Not "spankings" or even "whippings" — this guy really beat us BAD!! Being the eldest, I caught it the worse.

Anyway, in 1957, while beating us with a rubber shower hose with a big metal head on it, he hit my little brother ████ right in the forehead and it cut him to the bone. They had to call an ambulance and the hospital called the law! Well, when they took us (3) boys down to the police station and talked with us, they stripped us naked and took some pictures of us with all kinds of bruises all over our bodies. Those cops got █████!! They put █████ in jail that same night and took us (3) boys to juvenile hall.

Well, █████ people had money and they got him off with no prison time. My two brothers went back with him & my mom but they didn't want me there no more. That was fine with me because I hated that man!! I hated & feared him BAD!" (OVER)

So, here I was, (10) years old and no place to go. I went to several foster homes in the next (2) years. None of them seemed to work but for different reasons. Finally, I was sent to the "Corvalis Farm Home "For Unwanted Children" in Corvalis, Oregon. I never forgot that one word: "Unwanted". I stayed there about a year and me and another boy, (14) years old he was, ran off and broke into a bunch of houses and tried to steal a couple of cars.

For this, I was sent to "McClaren School For Boys" at Woodburn, Oregon. This was a real "reformatory" and I was there for (18) months. I learned how to fight, smoke, cuss and all about girls there at "Woodburn".

In the meantime, my mom finally got tired of ██████ and she moved back to Jackson, Tenn., with her mom and took my (2) brothers & baby sister with her. When I got paroled out of Woodburn in 1960, I was almost (13) years old and I was a little "█████" juvenile deliquent. They paroled me back to Tennessee in the care of my mom.

Needless to say, I just couldn't re-adjust to the "free world". I was no longer happy just being a little ignorant Tennessee "hillbilly". I was a little ██████ — and in less than (6) months — we had moved to Lexington, Tennessee, where my mom started living with a man named ████████. He was the sheriff of that county!". (Later on.)

Anyway, pretty soon I got caught stealing and me and another guy, ████████████, got sent to the "State Vocational School For White Boys" at Jordonia, Tennessee. I was there for a year, got out and was back in jail within a month! (Smile) This time I was sent to the "Tennessee Youth Center" at Joelton, Tennessee and I was there for (1½) years. I joined the U.S. Marine Corps and went to Parris Island, South Carolina for boot camp, then to Camp Lejune, North Carolina for A.I.T. and then to Cherry Point, North Carolina, where I was stationed.

In Feb. of 1965 me and another Marine went A.W.O.L. and went to his home in Shelbyville, Indiana. We pulled an armed robbery and got caught. We got kicked out of the Marine Corps and got a (2) years to (10) years sentence at the "Indiana State Penal Farm" at Greencastle, Indiana. I was there (4) months and escaped.

I went all over Indiana, Ohio, Missouri, Tennessee, Florida, Mississippi, Mexico and finally here in Stockton, California. I robbed stores, gas stations, banks, department stores and stole all kinds of cars. Finally, on June 7, 1965, in Stockton, California, while drinking with a car full of girls & boys, all of us (17) & (18) years old, we got pulled over by Johnny Law, and all my robbing & stealing caught up with me. I got sent to prison for (20) years.

But, when I got to prison, all the

(OVER)

prison "gang wars" were going on. The Blacks had the "Black Guer-illa Family" (B.G.F.) the Mexicans had the "Mexican Mafia" (EME) and the "Nuestra Familia" (N.F.) and we whites had a group called the "Aryan Brotherhood" (A.B.)

Because I was (18) years old, born in Tennessee, ex-Marine and had some "heart" I was soon caught-up in the middle of some, exscuse my French, "serious ███". Between 1965 and 1967 I was involved in several stabbings and five killings. By the time I was (21) years old, I was on "Death Row" condemned to die for (2) prison murders. I actually grew-up on "Death Row". I was up there for (7½) years waiting to be executed. That's where I met Charlie.

Anyway, the death penalty was abolished in 1974 and I came off the "Row" with a death sentence commuted to "life imprisonment without the possibility of parole". I've been doing that sentence all these years. I've served over (40) years locked-up in my (49) years on this earth. I've done over (32) years solid without having been out for even (1) single day.

LeAnn, I take no pride in what I've done with my life. I've never hurt a woman or a child — nor would I. It's just not in me. But, I have done some serious wrong in my life and I'm paying for it. I'm not "snivelling" or "whining". I did the crimes and now I'm doing the time. But, you did ask and now you know. I'm not a very "nice guy" at all!!

I will say one thing in my behalf. I did all this wrong when I was a young stupid ▆ kid trying to be a "tough guy". I've committed no kind of serious crime since Nov. 6, 1969, when I killed another "tough guy" in a knife fight where he was doing his ▆▆▆▆ to kill me. So, for the past (28) years I've done no violence to anyone other than a fist-fight every now & then. Still, I did what I did and I'll continue to pay for what I did.

Look "Featherwood", my people raised me up in the Pentacostal faith. Though I don't live like I should, I will tell you that I believe in the Lord Jesus Christ and I pray to God that I'll be forgiven for my sins and that I'll not go to hell. I can only hope that God will see fit to grant me eternal life in a place far better than this place has been for me. Amen."

Okay, this has been a tough letter to write. A lot of bad memories. I've tried not to make excuses for what I've done and I've been honest with you because you wanted to know. It's not very pretty, is it? No, I can't say I'm very proud of what I've done. I can say that I'm sorry for much of what I've done, not all of it, and that I'd like to make whatever amends I can with what time I've got left.

Listen LeAnn, you bring a little sunlight into a pretty dark place. Take care and write whenever you wish. I am here and I am... Your Friend, Roger Dale ✳: ✳:

Let the wicked forsake their ways and the unrighteous their thoughts. Let them turn to the Lord, and he will have mercy on them, and to our God, for he will freely pardon.

(Isaiah 55:7 (NIV)

We know that men are saved by repentance and faith, and whoever does call upon the name of the Lord shall be saved. But salvation is a supernatural work of God that will always produce fruit. And the evidence, not the cause, but the evidence of salvation is a changed life, a changing life.

(Paul Washer)

LETTER 4

Roger Dale Smith
A-93198-C 4A-4R-57-L
Corcoran State Prison
Corcoran, California
                    93212

                                    Ms. LeAnn Redding
                                    P.O. Box # ▬▬
STATE
PRISON
CORCORAN   Sardis, Tennessee
                                                38371

3/18/97

Tennessee Girl:

I received your letter dated 3/9/97 in tonight's mail. It only took (9) days! That's pretty good, huh? Great to hear from you. I didn't get the necklace but I really do appreciate the thought behind it. They should send it back to you and, _if_ they do, maybe you could just save it and we can both play like I'm wearing it. What do you think?

Hey! your dad sounds like a really good man! Your quote about him on the church doors makes a lot of sense. It's funny you should mention the Methodist church. I was once a member of the "Methodist Youth Fellowship" in Forrest Grove, Tennessee! Yeah, I was one of the leader singers in the choir and really got into the "M.Y.F." activities of our church. My favorite song was, "He Arose." I don't know about a seat in heaven-to tell you the truth- I'd be perfectly happy to just get there even if it meant hanging on to some roots on a tree in heaven! (Smile!) Since I've made such a mess of this life here on earth I sure do hope & pray that I'm given even the lowliest of positions in heaven. 'Cause "Featherwood," I sure don't want no part of that other place!! If I were given a choice of ruling in Hell or serving in Heaven, girl, you can rest assured I'd be one of the happiest servants in creation! Though I joke about it, please believe me when I say I'm dead serious in what I say!!

LeAnn, I want to make a couple of things perfectly clear. 1) As a kid, (17) to (23) years old, being a true Tennessee Hillbilly, I _was_ a stone racist! And yes, I became not only a member but one of the leaders of the A.B.- and that was one of the absolutely dumbest things I ever done!! I'm ashamed of myself for having been so stupid even as a young kid. If you have any pull with ****, LeAnn, tell him to leave that "Klan" stuff alone! Speaking from experience, <u>anybody</u> that hides behind a mask and a sheet is a complete fool and a straight-out coward!! Yes, because of my upbringing, I still have some racist leanings which I know are wrong but which I can't seem to grow out of. I don't like to see a Black man with a White woman. It isn't <u>right</u> to feel this way nor am I proud of it in any sense of the word. Some people are going to get one big surprise <u>if</u> God should just happen to be Black!! But, leaving out the spiritual aspect of it, putting down <u>anyone</u> because of their race, color or religion is just plain not right. No one can help what they are. And what gets me the most is putting anyone down for such stupid, trivial reasons as what they are simply born into! I can't say as to how I could have much respect for such a man as ****. The "K.K.K.", <u>in</u> <u>my</u> <u>opinion</u>, are no better than any other terrorist organization. I don't cotton to their ideas nor the cowardly manner in which they operate- <u>Period</u>!! 2) The "Aryan Nation" is simply an offshoot of the "Aryan Brotherhood" and I'm flat-out opposed to their idealogy-Period!! What we do as young kids can, to some extent, be blamed on immaturity and simple ignorance. But, once we've become mature and attain adult status, mentally & physically, it's then time to put those childish thoughts & actions to rest. That's the hallmark of an adult- responsibility & accountability.

I think it's absolutely great about your choosing to join the armed forces! (Naturally I'd prefer to see you become a Marine than join the Army-Hah! Hah!) But LeAnn, to tell you the truth, maybe you could look into all of them real carefully before you finally decide because it is my understanding that the U.S. Navy and Air Force offer the very best of all our Armed Forces- including traveling around & seeing the whole world.

And, not to belabor the point, you'll probably never get a better chance to join the very best of them all-U.S. Marine Corps! It don't get any better!! (Smile!) The training is far, far tougher than any other branch of the service, but when you do get through "Boot Camp" you will <u>know</u>, absolutely and positively <u>know</u>, that you are the BEST!! It just don't get no better! A great feeling "Featherwood"!! And how does this sound? "Leatherneck Featherwood" Class, huh? Naturally I'm slightly biased having been, and will remain, a "Jarhead"!! Semper Fi!! Whichever you choose, give them your very best and you'll never be sorry.

Yes, I know a lot of people in prison. In fact, I truly don't know many people <u>not</u> in prison. (Smile!) And, yes, I do talk on the phone with my kinfolk. Yes, I gave Charlie your hello and he sends you his regards and respects- and he asks you to send him a picture of yourself when you get your "Spring" flicks, okay? Okay!! Yes, the flooding was also bad out here in Northern California. I, too, felt sorry for the people who lost their homes and businesses- especially the ones without insurance. Whew!

LeAnn, I'm glad you let your daddy know you love him. From all you've said about him, he really does sound like a real man and a great father. I hope you do get your car, but if you don't, give him a hug anyway and let him know you love <u>him</u>. It never hurts to tell someone you love them- because you can just bet that it will hurt him worse than you if, for whatever reason, he can't give his little girl something she truly wants. If that man could, <u>you'd</u> get a Rolls Royce or a Jaguar!! Think about it.

No, I can't have a rebel flag but, once again, I thank you for the thought. In fact, there isn't anything you can send me other than a letter every now and then and maybe a picture whenever you can.

Hey! check it out. Another young kid wrote Charlie and sent him a couple of poems. I'm enclosing a couple of letters he wrote. Even though he sounds kind of "rough" I think the kid is really a pretty nice kid. He does write some pretty good poetry- even if it is kind of "dark" or "brooding" in nature. I wrote C**** and told him about you. I <u>did</u> <u>not</u> send him any of your letters or poems. I did mention that you also wrote some nice poems and that you & I had gotten along pretty good. I asked him if he'd like to write you and I'm now asking you if you'd maybe like to write him. LeAnn, I think that this young man could really use a friend at this point in his life. I'm kind of hoping that you and he could become friends and maybe share some of your poetry with each other. I <u>did</u> <u>not</u> give him your address but I did tell him your name. As I told you before- "LeAnn" is truly a beautiful name. Come to think about it, "C****" ain't so bad either! (Smile!) So, read his letters and let me know what you think, okay?

Well, "Featherwood", I guess I'm just about through for now. LeAnn, as you grow older and your world begins to open up, you'll probably not have a whole lot of time for me- and I want you to know that this is only natural and I will not be hurt or angry with you. It is a real pleasure for me to know you and to have had even a little time to watch you grow from a young lady to a mature, stable and happy adult. So, don't worry about saying goodbye or figuring out how to tell me so long. Believe me LeAnn, <u>both</u> of us will know when it is time for you to move on along. Don't you worry none. I'm very much appreciative of what time I will have had to know you. So, in that sense, I, too, say …

Much Love & God Bless You

For Being You!

Roger Dale

3/18/97

Tennessee Girl:

I received your letter dated 3/9/97 in tonight's mail. It only took (9) days! That's pretty good, huh? Great to hear from you. I didn't get the necklace but I really do appreciate the thought behind it. They should send it back to you and, if they do, maybe you could just save it and we can both play like I'm wearing it. What do you think?

Hey! your dad sounds like a really good man! Your quote about him on the church doors makes a lot of sense. It's funny you should mention the Methodist church. I was once a member of the "Methodist Youth Fellowship" in Forrest Grove, Tennessee! Yeah, I was one of the leader singers in the choir and really got into the "M.Y.F." activities of our church. My favorite song was, "He Arose". I don't know about a seat in heaven — to tell you the truth — I'd be perfectly happy to just get there even if it meant hanging on to some roots on a tree in heaven! (Smile.) Since I've made such a mess of this life here on earth I sure do hope & pray that I'm given even the lowliest of positions in heaven. 'Cause "Featherwood", I sure don't want no part of that other place!! If I were given a choice of ruling in hell or serving in heaven, girl, you can rest assured I'd be one of the happiest servants in creation! Though I joke about it, please believe me when I say I'm dead serious in what I say!!

LeAnn, I want to make a couple of things per-
fectly clear. ") As a kid, (17) to (23) years old, being a true
Tennessee Hillbilly, I was a stone racist! And yes, I became not only a member but one of the leaders of the A.B. —
and that was one of the absolutely dumbest things I ever done!!
I'm ashamed of myself for having been so ████ stupid even as
a young kid. If you have any pull with ████████, LeAnn,
tell him to leave that "Klan" ████████ alone! Speaking
from experience, anybody that hides behind a mask and a
sheet is a ████ fool and a straight-out coward!! Yes,
because of my upbringing, I still have some racist leanings which I know are wrong but which I can't seem
to grow out of. I don't like to see a Black man with
a white woman. It isn't right to feel this way nor am I
proud of it in any sense of the word. Some people are going to
get one big surprise if God should just happen to be Black!!
But, leaving out the spiritual aspect of it, putting down anyone
because of their race, color or religion is just plain not right.
No one can help what they are. And what gets me the
most is putting anyone down for such stupid, trivial reasons as what they are simply born into! I can't say as to
how I could have much respect for such a man as ████
████████. The "K.K.K.", in my opinion, are no
better than any other terrorist organization. I don't
cotton to their ideas nor the cowardly manner in
which they operate — Period!! 2.) The "Aryan Nation" is
simply an offshoot of the "Aryan Brotherhood" and I'm
flat-out opposed to their ideology — Period!! What we do

as young kids can, to some extent, be blamed on immaturity and simple ignorance. But, once we've become mature and attain adult status, mentally & physically, it's then time to put those childish thoughts & actions to rest. That's the hallmark of an adult — responsibility & accountability.

I think it's absolutely great about your choosing to join the armed forces! (Naturally I'd prefer to see you become a Marine than join the Army — Hah! Hah!) But LeAnn, to tell you the truth, maybe you could look into all of them real carefully before you finally decide because it is my understanding that the U.S. Navy and Air Force offer the very best of all our Armed Forces — including traveling around & seeing the whole world. And, not to belabor the point, you'll probably never get a better chance to join the very best of them all — U.S. Marine Corps! It don't get any better! (Smile!) The training is far, far tougher than any other branch of the service, but when you do get through "Boot Camp" you will know, absolutely and positively know, that you are the BEST! It just don't get no better! A great feeling "Leatherwood"! And how does this sound? "Leatherneck Leatherwood" Class, huh? Naturally I'm slightly biased having been, and will remain, a "Jarhead"!! Semper Fi!! Whichever you choose, give them your very best and you'll never be sorry.

Yes, I know a lot of people in prison. In fact, I truly don't know many people not in prison. (Smile!) And, yes, I do talk on the phone with my kinfolk.

Yes, I gave Charlie your hello and he sends you his regards and respects — and he asks you to send him a picture of yourself when you get your "Spring" flicks, okay? Okay! Yes, the flooding was also bad out here in Northern California. I, too, felt sorry for the people who lost their homes and businesses — especially the ones without insurance. Whew!

LeAnn, I'm glad you let your daddy know you love him. From all you've said about him, he really does sound like a real man and a great father. I hope you do get your car, but if you don't, give him a hug anyway and let him know you love him. It never hurts to tell someone you love them — because you can just bet that it will hurt him worse than you if, for whatever reason, he can't give his little girl something she truly wants. If that man could you'd get a Rolls Royce or a Jaguar!! Think about it.

No, I can't have a rebel flag but, once again, I thank you for the thought. In fact, there isn't anything you can send me other than a letter every now and then and maybe a picture whenever you can.

Hey! check it out. Another young kid wrote Charlie and sent him a couple of poems. I'm enclosing a couple of letters he wrote. Even though he sounds kind of "rough" I think the kid is really a pretty nice kid. He does write some pretty good poetry — even if it is kind of "dark" or "brooding" in nature. I wrote ████ and told him about you. I did not send him any of your letters or poems. I did mention that you also wrote some nice poems and that you & I had gotten along pretty good. I asked him if he'd like to write you and I'm now asking you if you'd maybe like to write him. JeAnn, I think that this young man could really use a friend at this point in his life. I'm kind of hoping that you and he could become friends and maybe share some of your poetry with each other. I did not give him your address but I did tell him your name. As I told you before — "JeAnn" is truly a beautiful name. Come to think about it, "███████" ain't so bad either! (Smile!) So, read his letters and let me know what you think, okay?

Well "Featherwood", I guess I'm just about through for now. JeAnn, as you grow older and your world begins to open up, you'll probably not have a whole lot of time for me — and I want you to know that this is only natural and I will not be hurt or angry with you. It is a real pleasure for me to know you and to have had even a little time to watch you grow from a young lady to a mature, stable and happy adult. So, don't worry about saying goodbye or figuring out how to tell me so long. Believe me JeAnn, both of us will know when it is time for you to move on along. Don't you worry none. I'm very much appreciative of what time I will have had to know you. So, in that sense, I, too, say ... Much Love & God Bless You For Being You! Roger Dale *:

For the Lord your God is gracious and compassionate. He will not turn his face from you if you return to him.

(2 Chronicles 30:9 NIV)

God proved His love on the cross. When Christ hung, and bled, and died, it was God saying to the World, "I love you."

(Billy Graham)

LETTER 5

Roger Dale Smith
A-93198-C 4A-4R-57-L
P.O. Box #3476
California State Prison
Coecoran, California
                    93212

STATE
PRISON
CORCORAN

CALIFORNIA
STATE PRISON
CORCORAN

Ms. LeAnn Redding
P.O. Box #█
Sardis, Tennessee
                38371

38371-0053

Roger Dale Smith
A-931988-C 4A-4R-57-L
P.O. Box #3476
Corcoran State Prison
Corcoran, California
93212

LeAnn Redding
P.O. Box #**
Sardis, Tennessee
38371

January 21, 1998

Dear Featherwood:

Hello! I received your letter dated 1-6-98 on 1-14-98. I am very pleased to hear from you and I was also pleased that you did indeed remember me. I am sorry that you are in such a sad state of mind and I am wondering how all this came about.

The last letter I received from you was several months ago but you were in such a happy state of mind that your present state of mind really surprises me! You were on your way to Georgia and you were looking forward to that move. Now it appears that you either didn't move or you have moved back to Tennessee. Which one was it?

Featherwood, you are going through a lot of changes both physically and psychological right now. It is perfectly natural and I would encourage you to go ahead and express these feelings rather than hold them in. Since there doesn't appear to be a woman in your house right now maybe it would be good for you to try and talk to one of the counselors in your school. If that isn't possible or you would rather not do it, I can tell you that I am here and I have a lot of time to give to you if you want it. I am not "mad" at you nor am I "hurt" in any way. Before I ever wrote to you, I pretty much decided that I liked you and that I would try to be your "friend" in anything that might come up in your life.

LeAnn, I'd like to encourage you not to "judge" your dad too harshly. From the things that you told me in your first series of letters, he sounded like a pretty good daddy and was doing his dead level best to try and give you a happy homelife. I don't know what has transpired between the two of you for you to feel so negative now. I do know that "growing-up" is a very difficult thing to do and that you will go through some very difficult "changes" as you grow and mature into a healthy and sound adult. Very difficult indeed! But, LeAnn, it is that way for all of us. No doubt about it, my little friend, you are going to need a true friend to encourage and guide you through this very difficult period in your life. I sincerely hope that I am that friend you need because I do care about you and your happiness a lot. If I didn't, I wouldn't be writing this letter. In this latest letter you sounded as though you were desperate for me to write back and you thought that I wouldn't respond. I don't understand how you could ever think that! I am now, was in the past and always will be there for you.

Isn't that what "friendship" is really all about? Who needs a friend a that is only there for them when things are "good"? But, when things are "bad" they are long gone! I certainly don't want a "friend" like that!! Do you? But, "Featherwood", you know what is even better than a true and loving friend like that? Jesus Christ!! I tell you true, that is the one and only true friend that any of us will ever have. Yes, there are many people in your lifetime that will be there for you regardless of where you are and what you may be going through! But even these so-called best friends may let you down. That is the wonder and glory of our Lord & Redeemer Christ Jesus! Praise His very name forever & ever!!! LeAnn, Jesus is not just some name in a story that took place several hundred years ago. He is very much alive and He will always be there for us if we will but call upon His mighty name!! That is the only real person that you can absolutely trust in any given situation. He knows exactly what we go through in our everyday lives because He had to use the toilet just like us! He knew what it was like to sit and cry for hours & and hours because we felt so miserable. But, Praise God, all we have to do is call His name and He will be there with us!! That isn't an empty phrase nor is it an "empty promise" that may or may not happen. It is the word of God and His word cannot be broken!!

LeAnn, I can be here for you. I can read your letters and I can respond to them in the manner that I think will help you. I can and will be your "friend". Though I am limited in some things because of where I am currently at, I can still be there for you when you need me to be. But "Little One" Jesus is there (24) hours a day, seven days a week. And all you have to do is call out His name!! That is all! Leave the rest to Him!! It really does work LeAnn.

I don't want you to think that I am "preaching" at you or trying to "talk down" to you. I am not!! I am desperately trying to reach you with His message because it took years of prayer and big time misery for me to find out this simple truth. I don't want that for you. When you need help, when you need someone right then and there, Jesus is not just some answer--He is the only answer!! I believe this with all my heart and soul. If I didn't, I wouldn't be telling you this. Please believe me LeAnn; Jesus is Lord! And what a wonderful, loving God He is!! Glory and power to Jesus!! Praise His Holy Name!! Amen!!

Featherwood, no, I am not mad at you! I am not having any kind of negative feelings for you. I have told you over and over that I am your friend and that I am here for you. Please don't ever doubt me in my loyalty to you. At the same time, I sure wish you wouldn't refer to your daddy with phrases like "I want to kill him" or "I am close to going over the edge and killing him". That isn't you! LeAnn, you are a kid right now. You are approaching becoming a woman and you have a lot of things that are bothering you. Even though I don't know your dad and the only information I know about him has come from you, there is no doubt in my head that your daddy really loves you and that the feelings you are having right now are simply a part of your transformation from a child into a woman. Maybe you could sit down with your dad and really talk to him about the kind of feelings you are having and how much you need him to know and understand you as a person and as his only girl child. Is that kind of conversation possible right now? Will you please make the attempt to have this kind of conversation with him?

Since I was born a boy, it is literally impossible for me to know what a girl feels and how they think. But, I do know this much; my mother and father had (3) boys and only (1) girl; K****. I have plenty of other brothers and sisters because my biological father and mother subsequently remarried and they had other offspring. But there are only (4) children which were born to my mother and dad. And LeAnn, K**** was the apple of my dad's eye!! He thought that the sun rose and set on this girl child!! I pretty much feel that your dad is very much like my own dad!! Please think about this and let me know what happens, will you? I'd sincerely like to know how you approach this, okay? Okay!!

Featherwood, I'd really like to share something with

you that I haven't talked about with anyone special to me or my family. Okay? I have, in fact, been reluctant to talk with anyone that isn't related to me by blood. My mother, L*** (now K****) got pregnant with me when she was (13) years old. I was born when she was (14) years old. Since she was such a young child when I was born she gave me over to my maternal grandmother and she raised me until I was (8) years old.

My mother remarried a guy named W**** from Klamath Falls, Oregon. This man was very sick and loved to beat up small kids! To make a long story short, I ended up in a reform school and I have been in these places every since. Don't get me wrong, I do accept responsibility for the things that I have done in this world both as a child and as an adult. Now, looking back, I praise the Lord that my grandmother did have me in my formative years because that was a very godly woman and she drilled that belief into me as a child. In fact, I learned to read when I was (3) and she told me the stories of Jesus and taught me how to read with her family bible. Thank you Lord!!

So, if I seem to be talking a lot about Jesus, please bear with me because He is the most important thing in this world to me. As a kid about your age, I didn't want to hear about God or Jesus because everyone would think that I was a "sissy" and make a target of me. All these years I spent serving Satan, I never complained or reformed myself because he wanted me to do the things that I wanted to do anyway!! (Smile!) Now, about (8) months ago, I gave myself over to the Lord Jesus Christ and I am trying to serve Him in the same dedicated manner that I served the old liar. So, bear with me my little friend and let me witness to you about the Lord & Master of this universe we live in. Okay? Okay!!!

Well, I guess I can now close this letter and get

it into the mail this evening. Once again, I was very pleased to hear from you and I hope that you will continue to write me when your feeling "down" or "up". You, LeAnn Redding, Featherwood, are my friend and I care about you very much. If you need me, I am here and I will not desert you. I never have given my friendship to anyone and then took it back. I shall be praying for you and I sincerely hope that you, me and Jesus can solve your problems along with your many other needs. I love you kid. I'm sure your dad does too and I know beyond any doubt that Jesus loves YOU!! Praise His Holy Name Forever!!!!

Love You LeAnn
Roger Dale

Roger Dale Smith
A-93198-C 4A-4R-57-L
P.O. Box #3476
Corcoran State Prison
Corcoran, California
93212

LeAnn Redding
P.O. Box #■   January 21, 1998
Sardis, Tennessee
        38371

Dear Featherwood:

        Hello! I received your letter dated 1-6-98 on 1-14-98. I
am very pleased to hear from you and I was also pleased that you did
indeed remember me. I am sorry that you are in such a sad state of
mind and I am wondering how all this came about.

        The last letter I received from you was several months ago
but you were in such a happy state of mind that your present state of
mind really surprises me! You were on your way to Georgia and you were
looking forward to that move. Now it appears that you either didn't
move or you have moved back to Tennessee. Which one was it?

        Featherwood, you are going through a lot of changes both
physically and psychological right now. It is perfectly natural and
I would encourage you to go ahead and express these feelings rather
than hold them in. Since there doesn't appear to be a woman in your
house right now maybe it would be good for you to try and talk to
one of the counselors in your school. If that isn't possible or you
would rather not do it, I can tell you that I am here and I have a
lot of time to give to you if you want it. I am not "mad" at you nor
am I "hurt" in any way. Before I ever wrote to you, I pretty much
decided that I liked you and that I would try to be your "friend" in
anything that might come up in your life.

        LeAnn, I'd like to encourage you not to "judge" your dad
too harshly. From the things that you told me in your first series of
letters, he sounded like a pretty good daddy and was doing his dead
level best to try and give you a happy homelife. I don't know what has
transpired between the two of you for you to feel so negative now. I
do know that "growing-up" is a very difficult thing to do and that you
will go through some very difficult "changes" as you grow and mature
into a healthy and sound adult. Very difficult indeed! But, LeAnn, it
is that way for all of us. No doubt about it my little friend, you are
going to need a true friend to encourage and guide you through this
very difficult period in your life. I sincerely hope that I am that
friend you need because I do care about you and your happiness a lot.
If I didn't, I wouldn't be writing this letter. In this latest letter
you sounded as though you were desperate for me to write back and you
thought that I wouldn't respond. I don't understand how you could ever
think that! I am now, was in the past and always will be there for you.

Isn't that what "friendship" is really all about? Who needs a friend a
that is only there for them when things are "good"? But, when things are
"bad" they are long gone! I certainly don't want a "friend" like that!!
Do you? But, "Featherwood", you know what is even better than a true and
loving friend like that? Jesus Christ!! I tell you true, that is the one
and only true friend that any of us will ever have. Yes, there are many
people in your lifetime that will be there for you regardless of where
you are and what you may be going through! But even these so-called best
friends may let you down. That is the wonder and glory of our Lord & Redeemer Christ Jesus! Praise His very name forever & ever!!! LeAnn, Jesus
is not just some name in a story that took place several hundred years
ago. He is very much alive and He will always be there for us if we will
but call upon His mighty name!! That is the only real person that you
can absolutely trust in any given situation. He knows exactly what we go
through in our every day lives because He once manifested himself in the
physical body of a human being! He had to use the toilet just like us!
He knew what it was like to sit and cry for hours & and hours because we
felt so miserable. But, Praise God, all we have to do is call His name
and He will be there with us!! That isn't an empty phrase nor is it an
"empty promise" that may or may not happen. It is the word of God and
His word cannot be broken!!

          LeAnn, I can be here for you. I can read your letters and I
can respond to them in the manner that I think will help you. I can and
will be your "friend". Though I am limited in some things because of
where I am currently at, I can still be there for you when you need me
to be. But "Little One" Jesus is there (24) hours a day, seven days a
week. And all you have to do is call out His name!! That is all! Leave
the rest to Him!! It really does work LeAnn.

          I don't want you to think that I am "preaching" at you or try-
ing to "talk down" to you. I am not!! I am desperately trying to reach
you with His message because it took years of prayer and big time misery
for me to find out this simple truth. I don't want that for you. When
you need help, when you need someone right then and there, Jesus is not
just some answer---He is the only answer!! I believe this with all my
heart and soul. If I didn't, I wouldn't be telling you this. Please believe me LeAnn; Jesus is Lord! And what a wonderful, loving God He is!!
Glory and power to Jesus!! Praise His Holy Name!! Amen!!

          Featherwood, no, I am not "pissed" at you! I am not having any
kind of negative feelings for you. I have told you over and over that I
am your friend and that I am here for you. Please don't ever doubt me in
my loyality to you. At the same time, I sure wish you wouldn't refer to
your daddy with phrases like "I want to kill him" or "I am close to going over the edge and killing him". That isn't you! LeAnn, you are a kid
right now. You are approaching becoming a woman and you have a lot of
things that are bothering you. Even though I don't know your dad and the
only information I know about him has come from you, there is no doubt
in my head that your daddy really loves you and that the feelings you are
having right now are simply a part of your transformation from a child
into a woman. Maybe you could sit down with your dad and really talk to
him about the kind of feelings you are having and how much you need him
to know and understand you as a person and as his only girl child. Is
that kind of conversation possible right now? Will you please make the
attempt to have this kind of conversation with him?

Since I was born a boy, it is literally impossible for me to know what a
girl feels and how they think. But, I do know this much; my mother and
father had (3) boys and only (1) girl; ████████████. I have plenty of
other brothers and sisters because my biological father and mother were
subsequently remarried and they had other offspring. But there are only
(4) children which wre born to my mother and dad. And LeAnn, ████████
was the apple of my dad's eye!! He thought that the sun rose and set on
this girl child!! I pretty much feel that your dad is very much like my
own dad!! Please think about this and let me know what happens, will
you? I'd sincerely like to know how you approach this, okay? Okay!!

        Featherwood, I'd really like to share something with you that
I haven't talked about with anyone special to me or my family, Okay? I
have, in fact, been reluctant to talk with anyone that isn't related to
me by blood. My mother, ████████████ (now ████████████) got pregnant with
me when she was (13) years old. I was born when she was (14) years old.
Since she was such a young child when I was born she gave me over to my
maternal grandmother and she raised me until I was (8) years old.

        My mother remarried a guy named ████████████ from Klamath
Falls, Oregon. This man was very sick and loved to beat up small kids!
To make a long story short, I ended up in a reform scholl and I have
been in these places every since. Don't get me wrong, I do accept responsibility for the things that I have done in this world both as a
child and as an adult. Now, looking back, I praise the Lord that my
grandmother did have me in my formative years because that was a very
godly woman and she drilled that belief into me as a child. In fact,
I learned to read when I was (3) and she told me the stories of Jesus
and taught me how to read with her family bible. Thank you Lord!!

        So, if I seem to be talking a lot about Jesus, please bear
with me because He is the most important thing in this world to me.
As a kid about your age, I didn't want to hear about God or Jesus because everyone would think that I was a "sissy" and make a target of
me. All these years I spent serving satan, I never complained or reformed myself because he wanted me to do the things that I wanted to
do anyway!! (Smile!) Now, about (8) months ago, I gave myself over
to the Lord Jesus Christ and I am trying to serve Him in the same
dedicated manner that I served the old liar. So, bear with me my
little friend and let me witness to you about the Lord & Master of
this universe we live in. Okay? Okay!!!

        Well, I guess I can now close this letter and get it into
the mail this evening. Once again, I was very pleased to hear from
you and I hope that you will continue to write me when your feeling
"down" or "up". You, LeAnn Redding, Featherwood, are my friend and I
care about you very much. If you need me, I am here and I will not
desert you. I never have given my friendship to anyone and then took
it back. I shall be praying for you and I sincerely hope that you,
me and Jesus can solve your problems along with your many other
needs. I love you kid. I'm sure your dad does too and I know beyond
any doubt that Jesus loves YOU!! Praise His Holy Name Forever!!!!

                                    Love You LeAnn,

                                    Roger Dale

In him we have redemption through his blood, the forgiveness of sins, in accordance with the riches of God's grace.

(Ephesians 1:7 NIV)

You will find all true theology summed up in
these two short sentences:
Salvation is all of the grace of God.
Damnation is all of the will of man.

(Charles Spurgeon)

LETTER 6

Roger Dale Smith
A-93198-C 4A-4R-57-L
P.O. Box #3476
California State Prison
Corcoran, California
93212

STATE
PRISON
CORCORAN

CALIFORNIA
STATE PRISON
CORCORAN

CORCORAN CALIF.
U.S. POSTAGE

Ms. La Ann Redding
P.O. Box # [redacted]
Sardis, Tennessee
38371

2/24/98

Dear Featherwood:

I received your letter dated 2/6/98 and am answering it as quickly as I am able. I, too, enjoy your letters as you are a bright & vivacious young woman and have an extraordinary personality that just bubbles out of you!!

No, you certainly are not a "dork" nor do you look like one. Don't think of yourself like that because, in time, you'll lose some of your self-respect and that is not cool at all!!

LeAnn, let me say this. All men are different when it comes to women. Some men like tall girls, short girls, fat girls, skinny girls, large breasts and small breasts, smart & dumb girls. Were I back in your age group, I believe you would appeal to me because I have always liked slender, athletic girls with small breasts. Don't trip on it because there will be several young men in your life and it will be completely up to you to choose the man you want. Hopefully he will be a "born again" Christian and will be good to you. Maybe you will end up with another girl! (Smile!) You're just a little bit young for that right now but you're getting to that period in time when all these things will become a strong focus in your life. Featherwood, you've got your whole life ahead of you- don't blow it!!

In "boot camp" there will be a lot of different things you'll have to deal with and you've simply got to go through all this as it is simply a state of maturing and becoming a young adult. You will make some bad decisions that may really hurt you. But, we all do!! Every single one of us!! But LeAnn, if your dreams are to come true you must make Jesus Christ the absolute center of your life!! If you will only do this one thing, you will find your own personal life to be "the bomb"! Believe me my little friend, the only answer to a happy, peaceful, successful life in this world, and the next, is by making Jesus Christ the "boss" of your entire life!! I truly know this is a fact and I sincerely hope you will do this because it is the only answer to all of the difficulties you will encounter as you grow into a young adult woman.

And I want you to be happy and have a wonderful life here on this Earth. I look forward to you sharing the bad & the good with me as you mature. But, even more, want to see you in Heaven and give me a big hug!! What a fantastic life that will be! And what makes it even better? It is an eternal life!! Our loving God is a living God!! And, if we accept Him and make Him welcome in our lives in this world- He will have something for us that is beyond my ability to put into words in the next world! And, however fantastic it may be- He has straight-out promised it will be eternal- without end! Glory to God! Praise Him! Thank you, Jesus for that victory! "Death, where is thy sting?" Washed clean and without blemish in the Holy Blood of Christ Jesus, "death" has no hold on us children of Almighty God!! We are redeemed! We are sanctified! We are saved! Nothing could be better than being saved and living a life of joy & bliss forever!! I tell you girl, Jesus Christ Himself said that "He goes to prepare a place for us!!"

So, please LeAnn, please keep Jesus in the center of your own personal life and you cannot lose with Him in the center of your life. Regardless of what comes against you, Christ Jesus will be there to protect and keep you safe & sound in body & spirit!! And, when you do "stumble" & "fall", as every single one of us do, Christ Jesus is right there with you to make it right! All we have to do is confess our sin and ask for His forgiveness and He is prompt to forgive us and, in

His Holy Word, He will even "forget" that our sin ever happened! Glory! Amen?

Now, to bring you up to date on some other things. Charlie is back down here in Corcoran from Pelican Bay. Yes, we are indeed close friends and I pray that, sooner or later, he will accept our Lord & Savior into his heart & soul. I will continue to bear witness to him of the love & compassion that Lord Jesus has in His heart for Charlie Manson and any other person if they will but ask Him into their lives! Glory to God! Thank you dear, Jesus!! Glory!!

Well LeAnn, I guess it is just about time for me to go. Listen, I am glad that you call me "friend" because I truly do want to be your friend and you do make me happy. As I have said over & over Featherwood, treat your daddy with respect & love. Go to him when he is sitting and watching TV and simply put your arms around his neck and say, "I love you daddy. I don't want anything except for you to know I love you!!" You'll be surprised at what that little simple act will do in both of your lives!! Please try it, please!!

Your Pal,
Roger Dale

2/24/98

Dear Featherwood:

I received your letter dated 2/6/98 and am answering it as quickly as I am able. I, too, enjoy your letters as you are a bright & vivacious young woman and have an extraordinary personality that just bubbles out of you!!

No, you certainly are not a "dork" nor do you look like one. Don't think of yourself like that because, in time, you'll lose some of your self-respect and that is not cool at all!!

Anyway, let me say this. All men are different when it comes to women. Some men like tall girls, short girls, fat girls, skinny girls, large breasts and small breasts, smart & dumb girls. Were I back in your age group, I believe you would appeal to me because I have always liked slender athletic girls with small breasts. (███████████ ███████ Smile!) Don't trip on it because there will be several young men in your life, and it will be completely up to you to choose the man you want. Hopefully he will be a "born again" christian and will be good to you. Maybe you will end up with another girl! (Smile!) Your just a little bit young for that right now but your

(OVER)

①

getting to that period in time when all these things will become a strong focus in your life. Featherwood, you've got your whole life ahead of you, I don't blow it!! In "boot camp" there will be a lot of different things you'll have to deal with and you've simply got to go through all this as it is simply a state of maturing and becoming a young adult. You will make some bad decisions that may really hurt you. But, we all do!! Every single one of us!! But LeAnn, if your dreams are to come true you must make Jesus Christ the absolute center of your life! If you will only do this one thing, you will find your own personal life to be "the bomb"! Believe me, my little friend, the only answer to a happy, peaceful, successful life in this world, and the next, is by making Jesus Christ the "boss" of your entire life!! I truly know this is a fact and I sincerely hope you will do this because it is the only answer to all of the difficulties you will encounter as you grow into a young adult woman. And I want you to be happy and have a wonderful life here on this Earth. I look forward to you sharing the bad & the good with me as you mature. But, even more, I want to see you in heaven and give me a big hug!! What a fantastic life that will be!

(2.)

(3)

and what makes it even better? It is an eternal life!" Our loving God is a living God!, and, if we accept Him and we let Him welcome in our lives in this world — He will have something for us that is beyond my ability to put into words in the next world! And, however fantastic it may be — He has straight-out promised it will be eternal — without end! Glory to God! Praise Him! Thank you Jesus for that victory! "Death, where is thy sting?" Washed clean and without blemish in the Holy Blood of Christ Jesus, "death" has no hold on us children of Almighty God!" We are redeemed! We are sanctified! We are saved! Nothing could be better than being saved and living a life of joy & bliss forever!! As tell you guys Jesus Christ Himself said that He goes it prepare a place for us."

So, please JeAnn, please keep Jesus in the center of your own personal life and you cannot lose with Him in the center of your life. Regardless of what comes against you, Christ Jesus will be there to protect and keep you safe & sound in body & spirit!! And, when you do "stumble" & "fall", as every single one of us do, Christ Jesus is right there with you to make it right!

(OVER)

4

All we have to do is confess our sins and ask for His forgiveness, and He is prompt to forgive us and, in His Holy Word, He will even "forget" that our sin ever happened! Glory Amen?

Now, to bring you up to date on some other things, Charles is back down here in Corcoran from Pelican Bay. Yes, we are indeed close friends and I pray that, sooner or later, he will accept our Lord & Savior into his heart & soul. I will continue to bear witness to him of the love & compassion that Lord Jesus has in His heart for Charlie Manson and any other person, if they will but ask Him into their lives! Glory to God! Thank you dear Jesus!! Glory!!

Well, JeAnn, I guess it is just about time for me to go. Listen, I am glad that you call me "friend" because I truly do want to be your friend and you do make me happy. As I have said over & over Heatherwood, treat your daddy with respect & love. Go to him when he is sitting and watching TV and simply put your arms around his neck and say, "I love you daddy. I don't want anything except for you to know, I love you!" You'll be surprised at what that little simple deed will do in both of your lives!! Please try it, please! Your Pal, Roger Dale

Therefore, my friends, I want you to know that through Jesus the forgiveness of sins is proclaimed to you. Through him everyone who believes is set free from every sin, a justification you were not able to obtain under the law of Moses ...

(Acts 13:38–39 NIV)

God will never reject you. Whether you accept Him is your decision.

(Dr. Charles Stanley)

LETTER 7

Roger Dale Smith
A-93193   C-011
Acute Care Hospital
P.O. Box # 3456
Corcoran, California
                93212

Le Ann Heatherwood
P.O. Box #
Sardis, Tennessee

Dear Featherwood:

How are you doing? I believe you already owe me (1) letter and this will make it (2)!! (Smile!) So, <u>this time</u>, I'm ahead!!

News here? Well, I just got stabbed (15) times by (2) youngsters that claim to be "Nazi Low Riders"- just another bunch of kids trying to be "tough guys" and earn their reputation as the ones who finally killed me! It is really easy to see myself in these very same kids some (25) years ago. I know exactly why they did it and I'd have done the same thing all those many years ago with one exception- <u>if</u> it had been <u>me</u> back then- I'd have killed whomever it was I was told to take-out. It's a different world now! We, in here, call it the "Pepsi Generation"! A lot of flash & pretty colors but falls apart real fast under pressure. That was how my "old dead self" would have handled it. As it is right now, with my having been "born again" in Christ Jesus, I not only forgive them for having tried to kill me, but, Praise God!, I will pray for them to accept Jesus and know what true happiness, joy & most of all, "love" is all about! Because, LeAnn, they are living a miserable life right here right now- and <u>if</u> they don't reach out to Jesus- this next place is BAD! (HELL!)

I know I don't want any part of it and I've always been considered a bonafide "tough guy" by everyone. Well, my young friend, Ms. Featherwood, (get on with your bad self Smile!) I know I'm <u>not</u> going to Hell because my God, my Master, has told me so in His Word!! Glory to His Holy Name! Glory!! But, <u>if</u> I had any real doubts, like them, I'd get busy in reading the Word <u>right</u> <u>now</u>! Hell is nothing to play with.

It is horrible, vile, nasty and painful- but most of all- after seeing God on the "Judgement Throne" and beholding His majestic powers and brilliant radiance and his great love for those all around Him- a soul condemned to Hell will never see anything but what he could have had <u>if</u> only he had accepted Jesus as Lord & Savior!! Glory! And worst of all- <u>it</u> <u>is</u> <u>for</u> <u>an</u> <u>eternity</u>!! There is no probation. No parole. No appeals to a higher court. Once there- you will be there forever- period!! Now, LeAnn, <u>that</u> scares me badly! So, <u>if</u> I weren't saved, <u>if</u> I wasn't absolutely sure that I am/ was/ will be saved by the Grace of God and the Blood of Christ Jesus, you can bet your little pretty self I'd be in that Book every single hour of every single day. Hell ain't nothing nice!!

In the next week or two there will be a new book out written by a Mr. Ed George and the title will be, "To Tame the Beast." If you can get one, do so. If you can't simply tell me and I'll try and get you one sent to this address. I can <u>always</u> use a book (20) of stamps so, if you want to do something for me- send stamps!!

I did come up with one other thing you could do for me if it isn't a "burden". You mentioned having joined the National Guard and you'd be shipping out in June. If that's possible, do this. I hear that cartons of smokes are $5 or $6 a carton of (10) packs. If that is true, please get me as many <u>cartons</u> of Camels & Lucky Strikes as you can. I'll pay you the total price. Let's just say you got (20) cartons of smokes (<u>NO</u> <u>Filters</u>) at $7.00 per carton. I'd have a money order sent to you for $140.00 to cover your cost. Then (5) cartons at a time, you could send me in a "care package" until you sent them all to me. In here, smokes are $27.00 a carton "name brand" and $23.00 a carton generic. I spend most of my money each month on smokes and coffee. I smoke about (4) cartons a month and I drink about (4) 12 oz.

jars, plastic jars of Folger's instant each month. At the base "PX" where you'll be going you could really, really help me out if you'd price check this stuff out for me and let me know.

Hey, LeAnn, got to roll! I do care about you a great deal little sis so please continue to write when you can. Give your mom & dad a big hug and tell them you really love them. Believe me girl, it will mean more to them than diamonds. It's true! Try it!

Love You,

Roger Dale

P.S.

How far is Huntingdon, Tennessee from Sardis? Also, how far is Sardis from Jackson, Milan & Skullbone, Tennessee? I've lived in all these towns but I was too young to remember them. But I do think they are pretty much grouped right there together. I also lived in Ripton, Foelton, Jordonia, Trenton, Lexington, and Forrest Grove & Shelbyville. But the only one I remember real good is Lexington. My mom dated the Sheriff! His name was R****! She also dated a judge! His name was C****- I think. Not really sure on that one.

OKay-girl-OKay!!

Later

Roger Dale

The Rock

4/2/98

Dear Featherwood:

How are you doing? I believe you already owe me (1) letter and this will make it (2) !! (Smile!) So, this time, I'm ahead!! :-)

News here? Well, I just got stabbed (15) times by (2) youngsters that claim to be "Nazi Low Riders" — just another bunch of kids trying to be "tough guys" and earn their reputation as the ones who finally killed me! It is really easy to see myself in these very same kids some (25) years ago. I know exactly why they did it and I'd have done the same thing all those many years ago with one exception — if it had been me back then — I'd have killed whomever it was as was told to take-out. It's a different world now! We, in here, call it the "Pepsi Generation"! A lot of flash & pretty colors but falls apart real fast under pressure. That was how my "old dead self" would have handled it. As it is right now, with my having been "born again" in Christ Jesus, I not only forgive them for having tried to kill me, but, Praise God!, I will pray for them to accept Jesus and know what true happiness, joy & most of all, "love" is all about! Because, LeAnn, they are living a miserable life right here right now — and if they don't reach out to Jesus — the next place is BAD! (HELL!) (OVER)

② I know I don't want any part of it and have always been considered a bonafide "tough guy" by everyone. Well, my young friend, Ms. Featherwood, (get on with your bad self ~smile!) I know I'm not going to Hell because my God, my Master, has told me so in His Word!! Glory to His Holy Name! Glory!! But, if I had any real doubts, like them, I'd get busy in reading the Word right now! Hell is nothing to play with. It is horrible, vile, nasty and painful — but most of all — after seeing God on the "Judgement Throne" and beholding His majestic powers and brilliant radiance and his great love for those all around Him, — a soul condemned to Hell will never see anything but what he could have had if only he had accepted Jesus as Lord & Savior!! Glory! And worst of all — it is for an eternity!! There is no probation. No parole. No appeals to a higher court. Once there you will be there forever — period!! Now, Le Ann, that scares the ███ out of me — pardon my French! So, if I weren't saved, if I wasn't absolutely sure that I am/was) will be saved by the Grace of God and the Blood of Christ Jesus, you can bet your little pretty ███ I'd be in that Book every single hour of every single day. Hell ain't nothing nice!!

In the next week or two there will be a new book out written by a Mr. Ed George and the title will be, "To Name The Beast". If you can get one, do so. If you can't simply tell me and I'll try and get you one sent to this address. I can always use a book (20) of stamps so, if you want to do something for me — send stamps!
(20)

③ I did come up with one other thing you could do for me if it isn't a "burden". You mentioned having joined the National Guard and you'd be shipping out in June. If that's possible, do this. I hear that cartons of smokes are $5 or $6 a carton of (10) packs. If that is true, please get me as many cartons of Camels & Lucky Strikes as you can. I'll pay you the total price. Let's just say you got (20) cartons of smokes (NO FILTERS) at $7.00 per carton. I'd have a money order sent to you for $140.00 to cover your cost. Then, (5) cartons at a time, you could send me in a "care package" until you sent them all to me. Down here, smokes are $27.00 a carton "name brand" and $23.00 a carton generic. I spend most of my money each month on smokes and coffee. I smoke about (4) Cartons a month and I drink about (4) 12 oz. jars, plastic jars of Folger's instant each month. At the base "PX" where you'll be going you could really, really help me out if you'd price check this stuff out for me and let me know.

Hey Le Ann, got to roll! I do care about you a great deal little sis so please continue to write when you can. Give your mom & dad a big hug and tell them you really love them. Believe me girl, it will mean more to them than diamonds. It's true! Try it!
Love You, Roger Dale ✳

(OVER)

④

How far is Huntingdon, Tennessee from Sardis? Also, how far is Sardis from Jackson, Milan + Skullbone, Tennessee? I've lived in all these towns but I was too young to remember them. But, I do think they are pretty much grouped right there together. I also lived in Ripton, Joelton, Jordonia, Trenton, Lexington, and Forrest Grove + Shelbyville. But the only one I remember real good is Lexington. My mom dated the sheriff! His name was ██████████! She also dated a judge! His name was ████████████ — I think. Not real sure on that one.

Okay — girl — Okay!!

Later

Roger Dale —

—— The Rock ——

*Whoever conceals their sins does not prosper,
but the one who confesses and renounces them
finds mercy.*

(Proverbs 28:13 NIV)

Jesus is not one of many ways to approach God, nor is He the best of several ways; He is the only way.

(A. W. Tozer)

LETTER 8

Roger Dale Smith
A-93198-C   C-011
Acute Care Hospital
P.O. Box # 5246
Corcoran, California
                93212

STATE
PRISON
CORCORAN

Ms. Le Anne Redding
P.O. Box # ■
Sardis, Tennessee
              38371

4/26/98

LeAnn:

I was trying to get everything in order to answer your letter of 4/13/98 because what you said on page (2) of your letter fitted perfect with what I was fixing to send you woman!! I mean perfect!! I'm enclosing that page of your letter to show you how it all "came together" on the very same day! (Smile!) I received your letters and Ed George's letter on the very same day-and the contents of each matched-up almost perfectly!! Cool, huh? Hah!!

Now, to answer your questions as well as I can. You can pretty well answer all of your questions with the information I sent to you. Seriously, every one of your questions were addressed in the things I sent you as "#2". This body would have been unneeded & I could have time & exspense! Hah!

"Featherwood", other than some stamps every now & then, you really can't send me anything at all. Why? Because that is how it is. In the "old days" (50's & 60's) you could just send a man a carton of smokes and a couple of chunks of homemade "fudge". Man! I <u>really</u>, <u>really</u>, <u>really</u> <u>LOVED</u> fudge!! REALLY! But, you just can't do that now. Besides, your just a kid and it wouldn't be right. But, I <u>do</u> thank you for asking me. That was really, really nice of you! (Smile!)

Love Ya Featherwood,
Roger Dale

4/26/98

Le Ann:

I was trying to get everything in order to answer your letter of 4/13/98 because what you said on page (2) of your letter fitted perfect with what I was fixing to send you "woman." I mean perfect!! I'm enclosing that page of your letter to show you how it all "came together" on the very same day! (Smile!) I received your letters and Ed George's letter on the very same day — and the contents of each matched-up almost perfectly!! Cool, huh? Hah!

Now, to answer your questions as well as I can. You can pretty well answer all of your questions with the information I sent to you. Seriously, every one of your questions were addressed in the things I sent to you as "#2". This body would have been unneeded + I could have time & expense! Hah!

"Featherwood", other than some stamps every now + then, you really can't send me anything at all. Why? Because that is how it is. In the "old days" (50's & 60's) you could just send a man a carton of smokes and a couple of chunks of home-made "fudge". Man! I really, really, really LOVED fudge!! REALLY! But, you just can't do that now. Besides, your just a kid and it wouldn't be right. But, I do thank you for asking me. That was really, really nice of You! (Smile!)

Love Ya Featherwood,
Roger Dale

LeAnn Featherwood
P.O. Box ■
Sardis, TN 38371

Roger Dale Smith
A-93198 C-011
Acute Care Hospital
P.O. Box # 3456
Corcoran, California
                    93212

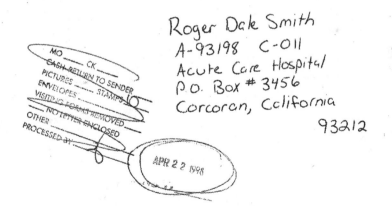

MO ____ CK ____
CASH___RETURN TO SENDER
PICTURES _____ STAMPS
ENVELOPES
VISITING FORMS REMOVED
____ NO LETTER ENCLOSED
OTHER
PROCESSED BY

APR 2 2 1998

The other day I read an article in the March 24th issue of "The Globe." In it was an interview with Mr. Ed George. It was entitled "Why Charles Manson Killed Sharon Tate." In the interview it says Charlie killed Sharon because her back porch was made of redwood! Can you believe it! I have never heard such idiotic lies in my life! I thought I was going to bust a gut laughing so hard! Anyway, the article said Mr. George was writing this book. I was wondering if it would tell the truth. Do you think you will be in the book? I think that would be so neat! The next time I am in Jackson, I'll go to the bookstore and buy it. (Jackson has the only bookstore around.)

Also, I will do my best about the stamps and a carton of smokes! I would send you some right now if I could. But my dad ain't around right now. It is just us three kids.

On the distances, I only know a few. Lexington — Sardis : 20 miles, Jackson — Sardis : 50 miles, Milan — Sardis : 55 to 60 miles. I'm not sure on the others.

For God so loved the world that he gave his one and only Son, that whoever believes in him shall not perish but have eternal life. For God did not send his Son into the world to condemn the world, but to save the world through him.

(John 3:16–17 NIV)

When we come to the end of ourselves, we come to the beginning of God.

(Billy Graham)

LETTER 9

Roger Dale Smith
A-93198-C   4A-4R-2 CALIFORNIA
P.O. Box #3467   STATE PRISON
                   CORCORAN
Corcoran, California
              93212

Ms. Le Ann Redding

Lexington, Tennessee
                    38351

10/1/98

Featherwood,

Hi! You mentioned in your letter with your picture in your uniform in it, that you'd written (2) letters to me. Well, LeAnn, I only got this one letter with your picture in it.

Secondly, you wrote that maybe I didn't want to write you any more. That is foolish for you to think like that! You are my friend! There is absolutely no way I wouldn't write you unless you told me not to.

I'm sorry that I didn't respond to your letter earlier but I couldn't. Me and Charlie got locked-up in the "hole" for "illegal business dealings" which we didn't do, but we didn't get our personal property until just a couple of days ago. Part of my property was my address book. Now that I have it, I can write you and I'm doing just that.

In fact, I'd like to ask a big favor for me. A couple of months ago I called my mom to talk with her. She lives with my sister and I can only call her once a month. But, when I called her, both she and my sister weren't there. Instead, my little brother took the phone call. From the time he was born until he was (16) years old, I never got to see or talk with him at all. Then, when he was (16), I got to visit with him at San Quentin for (2) hours. From that time, (22) years ago until a couple of months ago, I never saw him, wrote to him or been able to call him until he took that call at my sister's house a couple of months ago. He (his name is T****) and I talked on the phone for (1) hour and (15) minutes. He told me over & over again, at least (6) or (7) times, that he would pay my sister whatever the phone bill came to for our phone, (5) or (6) or (7) times calls.

Now, when I tried to call my mom last month, my sister had a "block" on her phone which wouldn't take any "collect" calls. Since I can only call "collect", there was no way I can call her or my mom and explain what took place when I called my brother. And since I don't have my sister's address I can't contact my mom or my sister. Now, I'm assuming that T**** (my little brother) <u>didn't</u> tell my sister or mom about he and I talking on her phone for (1) hour and (15) minutes and <u>didn't</u> pay her whatever the charges were. I don't <u>know</u> that this is what happened but that seems to be what happened because my sister put a "block" on her phone and I can't think of any other reason for her to do that.

So, Featherwood, I'd like <u>you</u> to call my mother, her name is K****, and explain to her exactly what happened when T**** and I talked on her phone. Her phone number (my sister's phone) is ***-***-****.

<u>Please</u> tell my mom & sister that I asked my brother over & over & over again that he would pay for the phone bill that he & I ran up on her phone and he promised me over & over & over again he would pay my sister whatever the charges were.

This whole thing wasn't my fault because he <u>promised me</u> over & over & over again that he'd pay my sister whatever the charges were on her phone bill. And, because I've lost her address and couldn't write and tell her about this, this whole thing has really got me feeling terrible. There is <u>no way</u> I would have called him over & over like that for (1) hour and (15) minutes if he had not promised me over and over again he would pay my sister what the charges were. <u>No way</u>!! I really, really feel bad about this and I'm absolutely furious at my little brother for putting me in a cross like this with my mother & sister!!

So, LeAnn, please do this for me, okay? Okay!! I

truly feel terrible about this and I want my mom & sis to know exactly what happened and how it happened. It still makes me <u>furious</u> just thinking about it!! I am really mad at my brother.

LeAnn, I'm sorry to "dump" this on you but I can't think of any other way of doing this as I can't call because of the "block" on her phone and I've lost her address so I can't write and tell her what happened.

I'll write again when I receive your reply to this letter. I am depressed about this whole thing and it just won't get any better until my mom & sis <u>know</u> what happened & how it happened. It is a terrible, terrible feeling and I want it over with!!

I sure hope that I haven't "bum-kicked" you! I think a whole lot about you and I wouldn't want you to feel bad. You are my friend LeAnn and I obviously trust you whole of a lot! God bless & keep you & yours safe & secure.
(***-***-****)
My Sister

Your pal always,
Roger Dale

P.S.
You really look great in your uniform! May I keep this picture of you? Let me know!

10/1/98

Featherwood,

Hi! You mentioned in your letter with your picture in your uniform in it, that you'd written (2) letters to me. Well, JeAnn, I only got this one letter with your picture in it.

Secondly, you wrote that maybe I didn't want to write you any more. That is foolish for you to think like that! You are my friend! There is absolutely no way I wouldn't write you unless you told me not to.

I'm sorry that I didn't respond to your letter earlier but I couldn't. Me and Charlie got locked-up in the "hole" for "illegal business dealings" which we didn't do, but we didn't get our personal property until just a couple of days ago. Part of my property was my address book. Now that I have it, I can write you and I'm doing just that.

In fact, I'd like to ask a big favor for me. A couple of months ago I called my mom to talk with her. She lives with my sister ████████ and I can only call her once a month. But, when I called her, both she and my sister weren't there. Instead, my little brother took the phone call. From the time he was born until he was (16) years old, I never got to see or talk with him at all. Then, when he was (16), I got to visit with him at San Quentin for (2) hours. From that time, (22) years ago

(OVER)

until a couple of months ago, I never saw him, wrote to him or been able to call him until he took that call at my sister's house a couple of months ago. He (his name is ████████) and I talked on the phone for (1) hour and (15) minutes. He told me over & over again, at least (6) or (7) times, that he would pay my sister whatever the phone bill came to for our phone, (5) or (6) or (7) times, calls.

Now, when I tried to call my mom last month, my sister had a "block" on her phone which wouldn't take any "collect" calls. Since I can only call "collect", there was no way I can call her or my mom and explain what took place when I called ████████ and since I don't have my sister's address I can't contact my mom or my sister. Now, I'm assuming that ████████ (my little brother) didn't tell my sister or mom about he and I talking on her phone for (1) hour and (15) minutes and didn't pay her whatever the charges were. I don't know that this is what happened but that seems to be what happened because my sister put a "block" on her phone and I can't think of any other reason for her to do that.

So, Featherwood, I'd like you to call my mother, her name is ████████ ████████, and explain to her exactly what happened when ████████ and I talked on her phone. Her phone number (my sister's phone) is ███-███-████ — ████ ████ ②

Please tell my mom & sister that I asked ████ over & over & over again that he would pay for the phone bill that he & I ran up on her phone, and he promised me over & over & over again he would pay my sister whatever the charges were!

This whole thing wasn't my fault because ████████ promised me, over & over & over again that he'd pay my sister whatever the charges were on her phone bill. And, because she lost her address and couldn't write and tell her about this, this whole thing has really got me feeling terrible. There is no way I would have called him over & over like that for (1) hour and (15) minutes if he had not promised me over and over again he would pay my sister what the charges were. No way!! I really, really feel bad about this and I'm absolutely furious at my little brother for putting me in a cross like this with my mother & sister!!

So, Le Ann, please do this for me, okay? Okay!! I truly feel terrible about this and I want my mom & sis to know exactly what happened and how it happened. It still makes me furious just thinking about it!! I am really ████████ at ████ (OVER)

③.

LeAnn, I'm sorry to "dump" this on you but I can't think of any other way of doing this as I can't call because of the "block" on her phone and I've lost her address so I can't write and tell her what happened.

I'll write again when I receive your reply to this letter. I am depressed about this whole thing and it just won't get any better until my mom & sis <u>know</u> what happened & how it happened. It is a terrible, terrible feeling and I want it over with!!

I sure hope that I haven't "bum-kicked" you! I think a whole lot about you and I wouldn't want you to feel bad. You are my friend LeAnn and I obviously trust you a ██████ of a lot! God bless & keep you & yours safe & secure.

Your pal always,

Roger & Dale

(██ → ██ ██)
(My Sis ██)

P.S.
You really look great in your uniform! May I keep this picture of you? Let me know.

(4.)

But God showed his great love for us by sending Christ to die for us while we were still sinners. And since we have been made right in God's sight by the blood of Christ, he will certainly save us from God's condemnation.

(Romans 5:8–9 NLT)

If I die without food or without eternal salvation, I want to die without food.

(David Green)

LETTER 10

Roger Dale Smith
A-93198-C   4A-4R-20-L
P.O. Box # 3467 (Ad. Seg)
Corcoran, California
              93212

STATE
PRISON
CORCORAN

Ms. Le Ann Redding

█████ █████ ████████

Lexington, Tennessee

10/15/98

Featherwood:

Hi! I received your letter dated 10/8/98 and postmarked at Jackson, Tennessee on the same date. As always, I was very pleased to hear from you. I've got a couple of things I'd like to share with you and I'd like you to take my comments to heart, okay? LeAnn, I would never do anything to hurt you in any way. It is very important that you truly do know beyond any doubts whatsoever that I'm your friend and would never do anything to hurt you! I mean this with all my heart and soul.

After I wrote you that first letter in response to your letter to Charlie, you wrote me back and, over the next (3) or (4) months, you and I just seemed to "click". As I told you in my very first letter, Charlie doesn't pay very much attention to 95% of the people whom write him. He normally wants me to read him any letters from "Family" members and to write them back whatever he wants to say about the things they wrote him about. So, he will get (40) letters in a couple of days and will only want to respond to (4) or (5). The rest, probaly (30) or more every other day, he will give to me to respond to or throw away. Even people who write a few lines of encouragement and send him a few bucks every now & then, he will very seldom even write a letter of thanks. To me, that is very, very rude! I used to get on his case about it because it wouldn't take but a few minutes for him to respond and simply thank them. But, a lot of time, these type of letters were written for other reasons that didn't have anything to do with kindness & generousity on their part.

When Charlie told me "why" they were truly writing

him "nice" letters and sending him $10, $20, or $50, whenever Charlie would write back to them and simply say "thank you", these very same people would take his note/letter, with the "postmark" to "authenticate" it down to various "auction houses", mainly "Sothby's" of England, and his autograph/signature with the "authentication" of the "postmark" here at Corcoran, would bring a "minimum bid of $300.00 and sometimes as high as $1,200.00!" I know this to be the absolute truth because I've seen it with my own eyes- many, many times over & over again! Don't ask me how & why his autograph is worth so much, but it certainly is to some people. Anyway, once I saw that Charlie wasn't telling me lies or wasn't just paranoid, I would just throw them away and ignore them most of the time.

For a lot of years, <u>before</u> I was "born again", I would pick out some letters that I thought I could "run a game" on and "hustle" them out of some money. Or, if they were women, I'd try to get them to come and visit me in whatever prison I was in. Then, <u>if</u> I were sucessful in "catching" them and could establish a relationship werein they truly cared about me, I'd take advantage of their feelings for me and, little by little, I'd get them to bring me drugs which I'd use some & sell the rest. Then I'd give them a couple hundred dollars a week, which I didn't need, and between emotional feelings and them needing that $ I gave them every time they came to visit, they were "hooked". These women were, for the most part, ugly, fat, on welfare, ignorant or some other "bad" thing- or they were just lonely women with no friends and no kind of love. Here they are coming to visit with some prisoner who will tell them all kinds of "good" things, and though they really know that the convict is "using" them for drugs and sex, they just want to be wanted, needed and loved; to "have a life". Sometimes, not very many, I would meet a pretty woman and, instead of drugs being my priority, I'd try to get a "love" thing going so I could have sex with her right there in the visiting room whenever we could get away with it! Or I'd talk her into taking some nude pictures which I would "fantasize" with.

Now, when I look back to those years, I feel terrible about the pain and shame I caused those people! If I had it to do all over again, knowing what I know now, I wouldn't do it!! Back then, I didn't care about the people's life I took when I killed them, nor did I care about the people whom I hurt, used and abused in every conceivable way you could think of!! <u>All</u> <u>I</u> wanted was to get/have the things <u>I</u> wanted. Nothing else mattered except getting what <u>I</u> wanted, when <u>I</u> wanted it regardless of the hurt & pain <u>I</u> caused others.

I tell you true, LeAnn, "Featherwood", Redding, I <u>know</u> that Christ Jesus died on that cross for <u>me</u>. I <u>know</u> in my heart that, having received Christ Jesus as my Lord & Savior, that <u>all</u> my sins were forgiven! Praise God for that! Thank you Lord Jesus for your sacrafice and your death on that cross! You died Christ Jesus so that we (me) might live- and not only live these few years we are in this world- but live forever & forever in the "home" you Dear Lord have went and prepared for us!! But, even though I <u>know</u>- not think- <u>know</u> that this <u>is</u> <u>true</u>, it is still extremely hard for me to believe that "Roger Dale Smith" is as "clean" and is as "pure" and is as "loved" and is as "saved" as anyone else whom has accepted our Lord & Savior Jesus Christ into their hearts, mind and body! Praise Almighty God!! Thank you Lord Jesus!!

(My other pen filler went empty on me a couple of minutes ago. (Smile!))

Yet, in an attack by Satan, he will try to destroy in any way he can that belief that Christ Jesus couldn't accept me/anyone because of all the terrible things we did before being "born again" in the blood of Christ Jesus. This is absoloutely a hard thing for me/us to accept because when people like "Mother" Teresa, Billy Graham, Kenneth Copeland, Pope John XIII, and other people in this catagory are compared with how I/us are, I/we just have too much "guilt" and sin in our/my life when those people seemed to have lived a "saint's life". But, Praise God, there is no truth in that! <u>All</u> of us have sinned and fallen short of what God demands of <u>all</u> his children. <u>None</u> of us can "earn" a place for us in "paradise"- <u>not one</u>!!

We are granted such a place only through the "grace" of God the Father <u>and</u> the blood of Christ Jesus the Son!! So, whenever I get to thinking of all the wrong that I've done in my life, all I have to do is get on my knees and bring it all to my Lord Jesus Christ- and- He will hear me, He will go to the Father and He will say, "Father, he is one of mine"!! Period!! Oh! LeAnn, what a kind, loving, mercifull and caring God we have!!

Look, I didn't get to really write you about some things that I wanted to tell you, and it is getting close to mail pick-up. So, to make sure I get this out tonight, I'll close this letter and write you another one to tell you what I meant to say in this one, okay? OK!!

Charlie and I <u>are not</u> "out of the !!hole!!" like you thought!! But, neither one of us did anything really wrong, so we should be out pretty soon now. It will be (30) days tommorrow (10/16/98). I also would like to ask a favor of you. In the "hole" where we are, we <u>are not</u> allowed to have postage stamps. So, I desperately <u>need</u> some envelopes and we can't get but (20) at any one time from any one person. I could use all (20) if possible- if not- as many as you can. Ok? Also, I'm sending you the envelopes you sent me in your last (3) letters, to let you see how they handle our mail. On the one sent back to you, I have absolutely no idea why that was returned. But, on the other (2) letters, (5) or (6) days ain't bad, huh? (Yes, yes, I know there "ain't" no such word as "ain't"!!) Also, I'm sending you some art work done by a friend of mine, a Mexican, who is also my Christian brother.

I know that your birthday is on the 24th of this month and I'm hoping you will receive the present I am sending to you. Yes, you are my "Lil Featherwood", my little "Tennessee Girl", my young friend, and I <u>do</u> like & love you as such. But, LeAnn, Jesus loves <u>you</u> more than anyone has or will ever love you!!

Much Love,
Roger Dale

10/15/98

Featherwood:

Hi! I received your letter dated 10/8/98, and postmarked at Jackson, Tennessee, on the same date. As always, I was very pleased to hear from you. I've got a couple of things I'd like to share with you and I'd like you to take my comments to heart, okay? Le Ann, I would never do anything to hurt you in any way. It is very important that you truly do know beyond any doubts whatsoever that I'm your friend and would never do anything to hurt you! I mean this with all my heart and soul!

After I wrote you that first letter in response to your letter to Charlie, you wrote me back and, over the next (3) or (4) months, you and I just seemed to "click". As I told you in my very first letter, Charlie doesn't pay very much attention to 95% of the people whom write him. He normally wants me to read him any letters from "Family" members and to write them back whatever he wants to say about the things they wrote him about. So, he will get (40) letters in a couple of days and will only want to

(OVER)

② respond to (4) or (5). The rest, probably (30) or more every other day, he will give to me to respond to or throw away. Even people who write a few lines of ~~encouragement~~ encouragement and send him a few bucks every now & then, he will very seldom even write a letter of thanks. To me, that is very, very rude! I used to get on his case about it because it wouldn't take but a few minutes for him to respond and simply thank them. But, a lot of time, these type of letters were written for other reasons that didn't have anything to do with kindness & generousity on their part. When Charlie told me "why" they were truly writing him "nice" letters and sending him $10, $20 or $50, whenever Charlie would write back to them and simply say "thank you", these very same people would take his note/letter, with the "postmark" to "authenticate" it, down to various "auction houses", mainly "Sothby's" of England, and his autograph/signature with the "authentication" of the "postmark" here at Corcoran, would bring a "minimum" bid of $300.00 and sometimes as high as $1,200.00! I know this to be the absolute truth because I've seen it with my own eyes — many, many times over & over again. Don't ask me how & why his autograph is worth so much, but it certainly is to some people. Anyway, once I saw that Charlie wasn't telling me lies or wasn't just ~~paranoid~~, I would just throw them away and ignore them ②.

most of the time. For a lot of years, before I was "born again", I would pick out some letters that I thought I could "run a game" on and "hustle" them out of some money. Or, if they were woman, I'd try to get them to come and visit me in whatever prison I was in. Then, if I were successful in "catch-ing" them and could establish a relationship werein they truly cared about me, I'd take advantage of their feelings for me and, little by little, I'd get them to bring me drugs which I'd use some + sell the rest. Then I'd give them a couple hun-dred dollars a week, which I didit need, and be-tween emotional feelings and them needing that I I gaves them every time they came to visit, they were "hooked". These women were, for the most part, ugly, fat, on welfare, ignorant or some other "bad" thing -- or they were just lonely women with no friends and no kind of love. Here they are coming to visit with some prisoner who will tell them all kinds of "good" things, and though they really know that the convict is "using" them for drugs and sex, they just want to be wanted, needed and loved; to "have a life". Sometimes, not very many, I would meet a pretty woman and, instead of drugs being my priority, I'd try to get a "love" thing going so I could have sex with her right there in the visiting room wherever we could get away with it. Or I'd talk her into taking some nude pictures which

③
(OVER)

I would "fantasize" with. Now, when I look back to those years, I feel terrible about the pain and shame I caused those people! If I had it to do all over again, knowing what I know now, I wouldn't do it!! Back then, I didn't care about the people's life I took when I killed them, nor did I care about the people whom I hurt, used and abused in every conceivable way you could think of!! All I wanted was to get/ have the things I wanted. Nothing else mattered except getting what I wanted, when I wanted it regardless of the hurt & pain I caused others.

I tell you true Jo Ann, "Featherwood", Redding, I know that Christ Jesus died on that cross for me. I know in my heart that, having received Christ Jesus as my Lord & Savior, that all my sins were forgiven! Praise God for that! Thank you Lord Jesus for your sacrifice and your death on that cross! You died Christ Jesus so that we (me) might live — and not only live these few years we are in this world — but live forever & forever in the "home" you Dear Lord have went and **prepared** for us". But, even though I know — not think — know that this is true, it is still extremely hard for me to believe that "Roger Dale Smith" is as Ⓗ

⑤ "clean" and is as "pure" and is as "loved" and is as "saved" as anyone else whom has accepted our Lord + Savior Jesus Christ into their hearts, mind and body! Praise Almighty God!! Thank you Lord Jesus!! (My other pen filler went empty on me a couple of minutes ago. (Smile!) Yet, in an attack by satan, he will try to destroy in any way he can that belief that Christ Jesus couldn't accept me/anyone because of all the terrible things we did before being "born again" in the blood of Christ Jesus. This is absolutely a hard thing for me/us to accept because when people like "Mother" Teresa, Billy Graham, Kenneth Copeland, Pope John XIII and other people in this catagory are compared with how I/us are, I/we just have too much "guilt" and sin in our/my life when those people seemed to have lived a "saints' life". But, Praise God, there is no truth in that! all of us have sinned and fallen short of what God demands of all his children. None of us can "earn" a place for us in "Paradise" — not one!! We are granted such a place only through the "grace" of God the Father and the blood of Christ Jesus the Son!! So, whenever I
(OVER) get to thinking of all the wrong that I've

② done in my life, all I have to do is get on my knees and bring it all to my Lord Jesus Christ — and — He will hear me He will go to the Father and He will say, "Father, he is one of mine"!! Period!! Oh, Jo Ann, what a kind, loving, mercifull and caring God we have!!

Look, I didn't get to really write you about some things that I wanted to tell you, and it is getting close to mail pick-up. So, to make sure I get this out tonight, I'll close this letter and write you another one to tell you what I meant to say in this one, okay? OK!! Charlie and I are not "out of the "hole"" like you thought!! But, neither one of us did anything really wrong, so we should be out pretty soon now. It will be (30) days tommorow (10/16/98). I also would like to ask a favor of you. In the "hole" where we are, we are not allowed to have postage stamps. So, I desperately need some envelopes just like the one you receive this letter in. They are called "embossed envelopes" and we can't get but (20) at any one time from any one person. I could use all (20) if possible — if not — as many as you can. OK?

(7.)

Also, I'm sending you the envelopes you sent me in your last (3) letters, to let you see how they handle our mail. On the one sent back to you, I have absolutely no idea why that was returned. But, on the other (2) letters, (5) or (6) days aint bad, huh? (Yes, yes, I know there "aint" no such word as "aint"!!) Also, I'm sending you some art work done by a friend of mine, a Mexican, who is also my Christian brother.

I know that your birthday is on the 24th of this month and I'm hoping you will receive the present I am sending to you. Yes, you are my "Lil Featherwood", my little "Tennessee Girl", my young friend, and I do like & love you as such. But, Te Ann, Jesus loves you more than anyone has or will ever love you!!

Much Love, Roger Dale

Featherwood
Lexington, TN 38351

Postmarked
10/2/95

JACKSON. TN 383
PM
08 OCT
1998

OCT 14 1998

I got it on this date...
five days! That is good!
(5) Days.
Pretty
dog-gone
good fe
2,000 miles!
(Smile)

20

Roger Dale Smith
A-93198-C   4A-4R-20-L
P.O. Box #3467
Corcoran, CA 93212

Featherwood ███████████
Lexington, TN 38351

POSTMARKED
①
(10/2/98) →

JACKSON, TN 383
PM
02 OCT
1998

20

②

Roger Dale Smith
A-93198-C   4A-4R-47-L
Box 3145
Corcoran State Prison
Corcoran, CA 93212

we got "five days.
that ain't bad"!

93212/3333

Featherwood

Lexington, TN 38351

I have no idea why this didn't get to me! It doesn't look like you did anything wrong to me!

Roger Dale Smith
A-93198-C   4A-4R-47-L
Corcoran State Prison
Corcoran, CA

My dear children, I write this to you so that you will not sin. But if anybody does sin, we have an advocate with the Father—Jesus Christ, the Righteous One. He is the atoning sacrifice for our sins, and not only for ours but also for the sins of the whole world.

(1 John 2:1–2 NIV)

There is no unforgiven sin on this side of the grave.

(Dr. Charles Stanley)

LETTER 11

Roger Dale Smith
A-93198-C   4A-4R-20-L
P.O. Box #3467 (Ad. Seg)
Corcoran, California
                    93212

" Featherwood "

Le Ann Redding

Lexington, Tennessee
                    38351

USA 32

LeAnn:

I don't know if I'm going to be able to get this letter finished in time, but I will certainly give it a shot! (Smile!)

In my other letter, I was going to explain a couple of things you might not like but which I feel should be examined. I was telling you all the nasty stuff I was doing <u>before</u> I was "born again" on 3/3/97, via the mail and visits. Now I don't do those type of things. I don't use any drugs that aren't prescribed for me. I don't "hustle" people. I don't try to get a woman as a "lover" type of relationship, I don't take advantage of people and I do my very best to witness about the love & mercy of my Lord and Savior Christ Jesus has for every single one of us who will simply beleive and obey Him. That is my biggest desire and I intend on giving God as much loyalty, duty & desire as I used to give Satan when I allowed him to run my life.

Since I've always had a special relationship with children and young people, those are the letters I now answer when Charlie gets through going over each letter to decide which ones he will answer and which ones he will give to me to answer or throw away. I thank God each and every time I am permitted to serve him in any way possible. We "born again" Christians are each given "missions" in the life to serve God. We may not "like" what we are given, but "like" has nothing to do with it! It is in the serving of God the Father, regardless of what the task is or from where we are given to go to do the work, that we derive the absolute joy & exultation we feel in serving God. LeAnn, it is my "mission" to "minister" and "witness" for Jesus from the maximun security prison from which I will never be released or paroled from, simply because God has given this to me to do- and I am honored to give Him service in any way I can.

So, I write to a lot of young people when they write to Charlie and he simply throws their letters away or gives them to me. These kids are usually pretty messed up mentally and they are reaching out to mass-murderers, cult leaders, satanists, etc. I write them and try to reach out to them in any way I can to become a "friend" to them. <u>If</u> they will let me become their "friend", in time, I may be able to share the love of our Lord & Savior Jesus Christ with them. Because they are kids, a lot of times they just need a person to hear what they have to say- and not "preach" to them or "talk down" to them or "order" them around.

You know what I mean because we've been writing for close to (2) years now. About a year ago, you were living in Sardis. You gave me a phone # to call you even though I told you we had to call "collect"- we weren't given the choice- it was mandatory to call "collect" or not call at all. Anyway, your dad got mad and put a "block" on the phone so that no inmate could call that number. (***-***-****). What is kind of "amusing" to me, whenever you would get a little "frustrated" or "angry", you'd write to me and "dump" those feelings on me. So, here I am telling you <u>not</u> to get mad at your dad, <u>not</u> to run-off, <u>not</u> to cause him pain but- just the opposite- go and put your arms around his neck and tell him you really do love him! Although he never knew it, still doesn't, he put a "block" on his phone to the only one (me) who was taking up for him and telling his daughter what would really be something she could do that would make her daddy very, very happy!! Weird, huh?

Then, about a year ago, you sent me a "goodbye" letter, told me you were moving to Alabama or Georgia to stay with your relatives and that I couldn't write you there because they wouldn't allow it.

About (4) months go by and you write and tell me you didn't move there after all and ask me to write you again. No problem! I did- and am still doing so to this very day! Then, right about (2) or (3) months later, you write and tell me about joining to Army National Guard in June and that you'd write me every single week so we could stay in touch and you could share your "boot camp" experiences with me. You don't write for (2) or (3) more months and I began to think of writing your dad and asking him if you were alright, but, I didn't because I didn't want to cause you any problems. Then you finally write and you're telling me your now staying with your mom there in Lexington where I used to live. You say you don't like Lexington and would rather be back in Sardis. I can understand that because Sardis is your "home town" and all throughout your life you will probably view Sardis as "home". Just like me thinking of Lexington as my home town and I only lived there for a couple of years. But it is "home" to me because, as a "free man" I never lived in any town for more than (2) years. And, "Featherwood", this ole boy is now, was then, and always will be a "Peckerwood" to the bone!! 100% "Pure Peckerwood"! Hah! Hah!

LeAnn, let me share something, a real sad story, with you, okay? Okay! At about the same time as you wrote Charlie and I responded to your letter, I was writing to (20) or (30) other young people. As I've told you many times before, your letter wasn't the kind that wanted an autograph or poem or song or picture or a lot of other things. If it had been, you'd never have gotten that letter from me. I would have simply thrown it in the trash where it would have belonged. But, instead of all that stuff I just now have written about, full of selfishness and other negative type of things, your letter was full of care, vibrant new life and compassion for Charlie. Though Charlie had put it in the ones he was throwing away, because it was from Tennessee, I read it and was really impressed with all the "positiveness" you had written- and- I just "fell out" when I saw it was from a young (15) years old girl!! You had also written a couple of poems which I really liked because they were vibrant, full of life and love instead of the depressing, ugly kind/type of poems a whole lot of young people write to Charlie. It simply took me a long time to see that the reason these kids wrote about such depressing, madness, chaos and violence & death, was because they looked at Charlie <u>exactly</u> how the "media", books, magazines, newspapers, radios & TV's had made him out to be. Some of these kids actually believed that Charlie had written "Helter Skelter" and in a couple of cases, they believed he had starred in the movie version of "Helter Skelter"!! I'm serious!!

And that is really sad. Regardless of what is taking place in a kids life, it is a terrible thing for these kids to find an infinity into the minds of Charles Manson, "Night Stalker" Richard Ramirez, and so many others just waiting for some young kid to step on the "web" they've spun out so they can cause even one more kid to mess him/her life up in this world- but- even worse is those same kids give their souls over to Satan.

Anyway, LeAnn, I was writing to some kids that were just some "good" kids and needed someone to listen to them and be there for them. One of them was another "Tennessee Girl" named K****. Like you, her first letter to Charlie was really a very nice letter and I responded to that letter just as I had responded to you. LeAnn, this kid had her act together! I mean she was really, really a beautiful girl with a pure sweet soul and it just felt beautiful to be around her.

I was transferred to the new pen they just opened up and (43) days later I was stabbed (13) times and went to the hospital for (67) more days.

So, I get back over here and I called her to talk with her about some things she and I were discussing at that time. Her mother, C****, took my call and I politely requested to talk with K****. C**** told me that K**** had recently died. LeAnn, LeAnn, that absolutely floored me!! It actually felt like someone had hit me extremely hard and I was "dazed"- out of it!! It just shook me up!

THEY CAN LOCK ME UP IN PRISON, AND THROW AWAY THE KEY, BUT THEY CAN NEVER TAKE MY FREEDOM ALL THE WAY FROM ME.

AS LONG AS I HAVE IMAGINATION AND SOME TALENT, SO IT SEEMS, I'LL ALWAYS HAVE MY FREEDOM TO DRAW AND ILLUSTRATE MY DREAMS.

10/15/98

Le Ann:

I don't know if I'm going to be able to get this letter finished in time, but I will certainly give it a shot! (Smile!)

In my other letter, I was going to explain a couple of things like but which I feel should be examined. I was telling you all the nasty stuff I was doing before I was "born again" on 3/3/97 via the mail and visits. Now I don't do those type of things. I don't use any drugs that aren't prescribed for me. I don't "hustle" people. I don't try to get a woman as a "lover" type of relationship, I don't take advantage of people and I do my very best to witness about the love & mercy of my Lord and Savior Christ Jesus has for every single one of us who will simply believe and obey Him. That is my biggest desire and I intend on giving to as much loyalty, duty & desire as I used to give SATAN when I allowed him to run my life. Since I've always had a special relationship with children and young people, those are the letters I now answer when Charlie gets through going over each letter to decide which ones he will answer and which ones he will give to me to answer or throw away. I thank God each and every time I am permitted to (OVER) serve him in any way possible. We "born again" Christians are each given "missions" in this life to serve God. We may not "like" what we are given, but "like" has nothing to do with it! It is in the serving of God the Father, regardless of what the task is or from where we are given to go to do the work, that we derive the absolute joy & exultation we feel in serving God. Le Ann, it is my "mission" to "minister" and "witness" for Jesus from this maximum security prison from which I will never be released or paroled from, simply because God has given this to me to do — and I am honored to give Him service in any way I can.

So, I write to a lot of young people when they write to Charlie and he simply throws their letters away or gives them to me. These kids are usually pretty messed up mentally and they are reaching out to mass-murderers, cult leaders, satanists, etc. I write them and try to reach out to them in any way I can to become a "friend" to them. If they will let me become their "friend", in time, I may be able to share the love of our Lord & Savior Jesus Christ with them. Because they are kids, a lot of times they just need a person to hear what they have to say — and not "preach" to them or "talk down" to them or "order" them around. ②

(3.) You know what I mean because we've been writing for close to (2) years now. About a year ago, you were living in Sardis. You gave me a phone # to call you even though I told you we had to call "collect"— we weren't given the choice— it was mandatory to call "collect" or not call at all. Anyway, your dad got mad and put a "block" on the phone so that no inmates could call that number. (■■ ■■ ■■) What is kind of "amusing" to me, whenever you would get a little "frustrated" or "angry", you'd write to me and "dump" those feelings on me. So, here I am telling you not to get mad at your dad, not to run-off, not to cause him pain but— just the opposite— go and put your arms around his neck and tell him you really do love him! Although he never knew it, still doesn't, he put a "block" on his phone to the only one (me) who was taking up for him and telling his daughter what would really be something she could do that would make her daddy very, very happy." Weird, huh?

　　　Then, about a year ago, you sent me a "goodbye" letter, told me you were moving to Alabama or Georgia to stay with your relatives and that I couldn't write you there because they wouldn't allow it. (OVER)

(4.) about (4) months go bye and you write and tell me you didn't move there after all and ask me to write you again. No problem! I did — and am still doing so to this very day! Then, right about (2) or (3) months later, you write and tell me about joining the Army National Guard in June and that you'd write me every single week so we could stay in touch and you could share your "boot camp" experiences with me. You don't write for (2) or (3) more months and I began to think of writing your dad and asking him if you were alright, but, I didn't because I didn't want to cause you any problems. Then you finally write and telling me your now staying with your mom there in Lexington where I used to live. You say you don't like Lexington and would rather be back in Sardis. I can understand that because Sardis is your "home town" and all throughout your life you will probably view Sardis as "home". Just like me thinking of Lexington as my home town and I only lived there for a couple of years. But, it is "home" to me because, as a "free man" I never lived in any town for more than (2) years. And, "Featherwood", this ole boy is now, was then, and always will be a "Peckerwood"; (4.) to the bone !! 100% "Pure Peckerwood"! Heh!

5

Le Ann, let me share something, a real sad story, with you, okay? Okay! At about the same time as you wrote Charlie and I responded to your letter, I was writing to (20) or (30) other young people. As I've told you many times before, your letter wasn't the kind that wanted a auto-graph or poem or song or picture or a lot of other things. If it had been, you'd never have gotten that letter from me. I would have simply thrown it in the trash where it would have belonged. But, in-stead of all that ██████████ I just now have written about, full of selfishness and other negative type of things, your letter was full of care, vibrant new life and compassion for Charlie. Though Charlie had ~~thrown~~ put it in the ones he was throw-ing away, because it was from Tennessee, I read it and was really impressed with all the "positiveness" you had written — and — I just "fell out" when I saw it was from a young (5) years old girl!! You had also written a couple of poems which I really liked because they were vibrant, full of life and love instead of the depressing, ugly kind/type of poems a whole lot of young people write to Charlie. It simply took me a long time to see that the reason these kids wrote about such depressing, madness, chaos and violence & death, was because they looked at Charlie exactly how the "media", books, magazines, newspapers, radios & TV's had made him out to be. Some of these kids actually be-lieved that Charlie had written "Helter Skelter" and, in a couple of cases, they believed he had starred in the movie version of "Helter Skelter"!! I'm serious!!

(OVER)

(6.) and that is really sad. Regardless of what is taking place in a kids' life, it is a terrible thing for these kids to find an infinity into the mind of Charles Manson, "Night Stalker" Richard Ramirez, and so many others just waiting for some young kid to step on the "web" they've spun out so they can cause even one more kid to mess him/her life up in this world — but — even worse is those same kids give their souls over to SATAN.

Anyway LeAnn, I was writing to some kids that were just "some" good" kids and needed someone to listen to them and be there for them. One of them was another "Tennessee Girl" from ████████, Tennessee, named ████████. Like you, her first letter to Charlie was really a very nice letter and I responded to that letter just as I had responded to you. LeAnn, this kid had her act together! I mean she was really, really a beautiful girl with a pure sweet soul and it just felt beautiful to be around her.

I was transferred to the new pen they just opened up and (43) days later I was stabbed (13) times and went to the hospital for (57) more days.

So, I get back over here and I called her to talk with her about some things she and I were discussing at that time. Her mother, ████, took my call and I politely requested to talk with ████. ████ told me that ████ had died on ████████. LeAnn, that absolutely floored me!! It actually felt like someone had hit me extremely hard

(6) and I was "dazed" — out of it!! It just shook me up

So now there is no condemnation for those who belong to Christ Jesus. And because you belong to him, the power of the life-giving Spirit has freed you from the power of sin that leads to death.

(Romans 8:1 NLT)

Faith in the Lord Jesus Christ is the foundation upon which sincere and meaningful repentance must be built. If we truly seek to put away sin, we must first look to Him who is the Author of our salvation.

(Ezra Taft Benson)

LETTER 12

Roger Dale Smith
A-93198-C   4A-4R-20-L
P.O. Box 3476 (Ad. Seg.)
Corcoran, California
                    93212-3476

STATE
PRISON
CORCORAN

Ms. Leánn "Featherwood" Redding

███   ███████   ████████

Lexington , Tennessee
                    38351

38351/1656   ║║║║║║║║║║║║║║║║║║║║║║║

11/6/98

Hello LeAnn!

I'm sorry that I stopped my last letter but I had to or I'd have started crying. You see, LeAnn, me and this young lady were really good friends. She was only a couple of years older than you and we had been writing for maybe (2) or (3) years.

You know what hurts me and makes me mad about this whole thing? This kid never told me she was going to die! She never even told me she was in a wheelchair and had a terminal disease!! That really hurts me because I didn't have a chance to witness to her about our Lord & Savior Jesus Christ!! Don't get me wrong, I always mentioned Jesus and how much He loved us, but I didn't get to "push it" because I thought we had a whole bunch of time left to build up to it over time! And we don't, "Lil Featherwood"!! We have got to "push it"- that's the one thing I've learned about this entire matter! Because she didn't tell me about her disease and because I mistakenly thought we had plenty of time due to her age, (17) when we first met, I didn't "push" Christ Jesus upon on her! I regret that more than anything else. I don't know if she died "saved" or not. When I called her and got her mother instead, I asked for K**** and was then told she had died. It just knocked me all the way silly!! I didn't know what to say and I'm a "man of words." Seriously, I am! I pretty much know what to say in any given situation, but this one here, flat-out "shut me down".

There was no way I could and/or would be able to reply to this grieving mother about her one and only daughter. And, before you know it I asked her mom, "K****" or "C****", I'm not sure how she spells her name, if K**** was "saved". That sure isn't something a person should say to a mother grieving the death of her one & only daughter. I felt so terribly "stupid" after I had asked her such a question. (I mean, LeAnn, what could the mother say if she answered? "Yes, my (1) and only daughter believed in Christ Jesus and he took her away." Or " No, my daughter is in Hell right now because she wasn't "saved" and didn't believed in Jesus.") But, in this case, her mother was very polite. She knew that her daughter and I had been writing for quite awhile and she and her child had sat down and talked about me for a long time on several occasions. Even though neither her or her child believed in Christ Jesus as "God", she did know that I was a "Christian" and that I'd talked with K**** numerous times on this very issue and that her daughter had told her that she really believed I was a "nice guy" and did believe in Christ Jesus as Lord & Savior of <u>all</u> of us!! <u>Everyone</u>, <u>every</u> <u>single</u> <u>person</u> that has been alive from Adam & Eve to the last persons on this planet, <u>EVERYONE</u>!! <u>All people</u>, shall bow their knee and proclaim with their mouth that JESUS CHRIST <u>is</u> LORD!!! He <u>is</u> worthy to be called "Lord"! <u>No</u> <u>other</u> can compare to Christ Jesus in glory, power and grace!! He <u>is</u> LORD!!! Thank you, Lord Jesus!! <u>You</u> and only <u>you</u> are worthy to be called "Lord"- <u>no</u> <u>other</u>- just <u>You</u>!! <u>Our</u> God, whether "Father Jehovah", "Christ Jesus" or "Holy Spirit" is a great "Living God" and He loves us so much, so much, so much!! Surely a God so great & powerful will have His great arms around this sweet & lovely girl <u>right</u> <u>now</u>. Praise God! Sweet Jesus, I pray that <u>You</u> precious Savior were right there with her when that moment came! In Your Most Blessed Name my Lord!!

LeAnn, I know that K**** mother is hurting <u>right now</u>! She just has to hurt so bad <u>and</u> <u>she</u> <u>doesn't</u> have that refuge (Our Sweet Savior & Redeemer) right. I thought <u>maybe</u> <u>you</u> could call her on a regular basis so that she could have that "girl thing" (mother & daughter) special relationship- and <u>you</u> could give her that "Jesus thing" which would surely give her some relief from that enormous grief & pain she must be in. What do <u>you</u> think LeAnn? Please don't "go along" with me for my benefit. Please! I'm asking you to be there for that hurting mother <u>if</u> that is what <u>you</u> feel? <u>If not</u>, please just tell me that <u>you</u> don't think this "witnessing" thing is you, okay? Okay!

Featherwood, never again will I not "push this Jesus thing" on some young adult or older child I'm writing. Never!! I've always thought I'd get to know the kid <u>before</u> I did any "witnessing for Christ Jesus" and run them off by being a "Holy Roller" to them. Most kids are attracted to men like me & Charlie for the <u>wrong reasons</u>!! Charlie doesn't care. <u>I</u> <u>do</u> <u>care</u> <u>very</u> <u>much</u>! Very much!! <u>If</u> I can't tell them about Jesus and how He has completely changed my life- and what He can do in their life- then I don't need to be writing anything else for that young kid. Charlie Manson is my friend. There isn't much I wouldn't do for him. But, LeAnn, Jesus Christ is my Lord, Savior and God! <u>I</u> <u>love</u> <u>Him</u> <u>with</u> <u>all</u> <u>my</u> <u>heart</u>, <u>soul</u>, <u>mind</u>! There isn't <u>anything</u> I won't do for Him. <u>Nothing</u>!

I do love you "Featherwood", I truly do. You're my buddy. My "Lil Tennessee Girl". But, LeAnn, dear friend, Jesus loves <u>you</u> so much more! Yes, He does. Glory! Glory!!

Me-
R.D.

11/6/98

Hello Le Ann!

I'm sorry that I stopped my last letter but I had to or I'd have started crying. You see, Le Ann, me and this young lady were really good friends. She was only a couple of years older than you and we had been writing for maybe (2) or (3) years.

You know what hurts me and makes me mad about this whole thing? This kid never told me she was going to die! She never even told me she was in a wheelchair and had a terminal disease!! That really hurts me because I didn't have a chance to witness to her about our Lord & Savior Jesus Christ!! Don't get me wrong, I always mentioned Jesus and how much He loved us, but I didn't get to "push it" because I thought we had a whole bunch of time left to build up to it over time! And we don't, "Lil Featherwood"!! We have got to "push it" — that's the one thing I've learned about this entire matter! Because she didn't tell me about her disease and because I mistakenly thought we had plenty of time due to ▓▓▓▓▓ age, (17) when

(OVER)

we first met, I didn't "push" Christ Jesus upon on her! I regret that more than anything else.. I don't know if she died "saved" or not. When I called her and got her mother instead, I asked for ████ and was then told she had died on ████ I believe she said and it just knocked me all the way silly!! I didn't know what to say and I'm a "man of words". Seriously, I am! I pretty much know what to say in any given situation, but this one here, flat-out "shut me down". There was no way I could and/or would be able to reply to this grieving mother about her one and only daughter. And, before you know it, I asked her mom, "████" or "████", I'm not sure how she spells her name, if ████ was "saved". That sure isn't something a person should say to a mother grieving the death of her one & only daughter. I felt so terribly "stupid" after I had asked her such a question. (I mean, Le Ann, what could the mother say if she answered? "Yes, my (1) and only daughter believed in Christ Jesus and he took her away." Or "No, my daughter is in hell right now because she wasn't "saved" and didn't believe in Jesus".) But, in this case, her mother was very polite. She knew that her daughter and I had been writing for quite awhile and she and her child had ~~had~~ sat down and talked about me for a long time on several occasions. Even though
(2) neither her or her child believed in Christ Jesus

as a "God", she did know that I was a "Christian" and that I'd talked with ████ numerous times on this very issue and that her daughter had told her that she really believed I was a "nice guy" and did believe in Christ Jesus as Lord & Savior of all ~~flesh~~ Everyone, ~~every single person~~ that ~~has been~~ alive from Adam & Eve to the last persons ~~on~~ this planet, EVERYONE!! ~~all people~~, shall bow their knee and proclaim with their mouth that JESUS ~~Christ~~ CHRIST is LORD!!! ~~He~~ is worthy to be called "Lord"! No other can compare to Christ Jesus in glory, power and grace!! He is LORD!!! Thank You Lord Jesus!! You and only You are worthy to be called "Lord" — no ~~other~~ just You! Our God, whether "Father Jehovah", Christ Jesus, or "Holy Spirit" is a great "Living God" and He loves us so much, so much, so much! Surely a God so great & powerful will have His great arms around this sweet & lovely girl right now. Praise God! Sweet Jesus, I pray that Your precious Savior were right there with her when that moment came! In Your Most Blessed Name my Lord!!

Jo Ann, I know that ████ mother is hurting right now! She just has to hurt so bad and she doesn't have that refuge (Our Sweet Savior & Redeemer) right. I thought maybe you could call her on a regular ~~basis~~ so that she could have that "girl thing" (mother/daughter) special relationship — and you could give

③

(OVER)

(4) her that "Jesus thing" which would surely gives her some relief from that enormous grief + pain she must be in. What do you think Le Ann? Please don't "go along" with me for my benefit. Please! I'm asking you to be there for that hurting mother if that is what you feel? If not, please just tell me that you don't think this "witnessing" thing is you, okay? Okay! Heatherwood, never again will I not "push this Jesus thing" on some young adult or older child I'm writing. Never!! I've always thought I'd get to know the kid before I did any "witnessing for Christ Jesus" and run them off by being a "Holy Roller" to them. Most kids are attracted to men like me + Charlie for the wrong reasons!! Charlie doesn't care. I do care very mush! Very much!! If I can't tell them about Jesus and how He has completely changed my life — and what He can do in their life — then I don't need to be writing anything else for that young kid. Charlie Manson is my friend. There isn't much I wouldn't do for him. But Le Ann, Jesus Christ is my Lord, Savior and God! I love Him with all my heart, soul, mind! There isn't anything I want do for Him. Nothing! I do love you "Heatherwood"

But, Yes He does. Your friend, Jesus loves you so much more. "Ol' Tennessee Girl". He does too, your my buddy. "Ol" P.S.

If we confess our sins, he is faithful and just and will forgive us our sins and purify us from all unrighteousness.

(1 John 1:9 NIV)

Atonement- (noun) Taking action to correct previous wrongdoing.
[1] is the method by which human beings can be reconciled to God through Christ's sacrificial suffering and death.
[2] Atonement is the forgiving or pardoning of sin in general, and original sin in particular, through the suffering, death, and resurrection of Jesus, [3] enabling the reconciliation between God and his creation.

(Wikipedia)

LETTER 13

Roger Dale Smith
A-93198-C   4A-4R-20L
P.O. Box 3476 (Ad. Seg.)
Corcoran, California
                93212-3476

CALIFORNIA
STATE PRISON
CORCORAN

U.S. POSTAGE
$0.32

STATE
PRISON
CORCORAN

Le Ann Redding

Featherwood:

Hello! I just now, a very few minutes ago, recieved your letter & (2) "religous tracts" dated 11/4/98! As always, I was very pleased to hear from you because your my little buddy! I'm of the opinion that you are under the impression on a couple of matters that are in error. I want these very small "differences" or "misunderstandings" (nice sized word, huh? Smile!) cleaned up <u>now</u>!

LeAnn, <u>I</u> <u>don't</u> think you are "dumping" on me. I don't know how or why <u>you</u> <u>think</u> your "dumping" on me. It simply isn't true that I think like that! Period! That's straight out ridiculous! Featherwood, you are <u>my</u> <u>friend</u>! I care about "my friends" a whole lot. But, I tell you true, your becoming more than a friend to me; your becoming like a daughter to me! My favorite part of this last letter you write me, (wrote me, yeah, I missed that one!) is what your brother did for you on that "prom dress" regardless of when the prom happens!

I'd like to shake his hand and give him a big ol' hug!! That's just great what that kid did, <u>especially</u> for his baby sister!! <u>Please</u> tell him I send him my regards and respect. I truly enjoyed coming to that part in your letter. To me, that is indeed an act of love!!

I had hoped that you would have received my present to you also. Since you didn't mention it, I'm assuming that you never received it. The man who wrote this last "Manson book", Ed George, is a personal friend of mine. He worked for the California Department of Corrections for (32) years before he retired a few years ago. I worked as his clerk for (5) or (6) years and we truly became "friends" but we both knew there was a "line" that neither one of us ever crossed. Since his retirement, we went through all the proper rules & regulations and now he comes to visit with me every (3) or (4) months. He can't afford more because I eat up about $20.00 worth of food and soda water every time we visit! Hah!

I helped him a lot in writing the book and I gave him a lot of pictures, at $2.00 apiece, which I paid for, that are in the book! Although it is primarily about Charlie, he does write about others, me included, and himself. I knew you went looking for it, I believe you even went to Jackson, Tennessee, didn't you? And you couldn't find it. So, I wrote him and requested that he autograph it and mail you a copy in time for your birthday. I wanted you to read it and let your folks read it. Then, I wanted to let you know how me & Charlie could sign it for you. With the pictures & the (3) autographs, you would have your car and a nice one at that! (Smile!) Now I've got to write and ask him what happened. Hopefully it will be done when he gets my letter in the next couple of days. Rest assured of this, I flat-out promise you'll get the book exactly how I told you! <u>Period</u>!!

Now, you'll know what happened with the other "Tennessee Girl" as I've had that sent for a few days now. In fact, I've been awaiting your response on that particular letter with anticipation. So, hope you've already written that letter <u>before</u> you even get this letter from me. (Smile!) It was a truly sad time for me because that kid was an amazing young woman. LeAnn, I sure wish you'd put her on your "prayer list". It is amazing how much her death affected me considering all the mayhem & murder I've seen and even, to my eternal shame, became involved in them personally. Yes, I know that I'm "born again" in Christ Jesus and am a "new" man! And Praise God for that! Thank you, Jesus!! <u>But</u> I also know that I'll <u>never</u> "forget" what I've done in this life.

Oh yeah! Back to "dumping" for a couple of minutes. <u>If</u> you have any problems or whatever it may be, and you need someone to share them with, I'm here for you. <u>Anytime</u>- <u>anything</u>! (I will put one "qualifier" on that. In deference to our ages & gender, I'm an "ol' fogee" on "sexual matters" and would not like to hear them from you or any other young lady- <u>unless</u>- there absolutely is no one else to go to that you believe will give you help. Then, come to me because I will help you out of <u>anything</u> I possibly can! That's a promise from me to you- and it won't every change in any way, shape or form. Okay? OK!!)

To answer some questions you asked I'll go right down the line, Okay? Here it is:

1) It's going sadly slow but we will make it! (Smile!)

2) Yes, me & Charlie are still in "the hole". It's been a couple of days off of (60) days now. And we truly didn't do nothing wrong- speaking for myself!

3) Featherwood, you don't have to apologize to me on the doggone envelopes! If you get some and don't care about them, cool! Send them! As for other things, don't worry a bit, I'll not ask because I know things are tough for a young person. Also, I <u>can't</u> call you while I'm in "the hole". Maybe I can work something out when I do get out. But I <u>cannot</u> call any way except the so-called "collect" way!! That isn't my fault. And I can't change it! I would if I could!!

4) I never for one moment didn't think you went to "boot camp". Seriously, I didn't. Yes, I knew you didn't go to Georgia, but I didn't care about it all that much. <u>If</u> you truly didn't want to continue to write me- that's your choice- either way! I keep telling you that you're

a young lady and you're going to change your mind about a lot of things until you mature. That's your privilege. That process is yours to do- we all go through that. And it is our honor & duty as mature adults to be there with you whenever you need us. That's what "love" is all about. Don't trip on this too much. You're not doing <u>anything</u> wrong at all!! Okay? OK!!

5) Here is another one from my Mexican friend Eddie. He, too, is a Christian even though he hasn't been "born again" he is definitely headed that way if I have anything to do with it!! (Smile!) (Big Smile!) I told him about your having written me some poems (I saved them but I can't have all my property in the "hole" so they are in my property) so he told me I could give you some of his stuff. Will do so every time I get a chance, Okay!! OK!! Maybe you'll send us some- okay?

6) I'll give Charlie your "Happy Birthday" wish. I'm sure he returns them to you. Also, yes, we both know you're not selling stuff we sent you. But, even if you did, I don't think it would bother us a bit. Once you've been given something, it is yours to do with as you like. It's yours!!

7) Last thing. Your letter is dated 11/4/98 by you. It is postmarked 11/4/98 in Jackson, Tennessee. I got it this date 11/12/98- so it must have taken (8) days to reach me. Not bad considering at least one weekend, (2) days, and (1) holiday (11/11/98).

Gotta go girl! I'm here for you. <u>Our</u> Lord & Savior did indeed "bless me" with bringing you into my life. Thank you, Jesus!!

Love,
Roger Dale

He & You are both
<u>My</u> <u>Friends</u>!!
11/12/98

P.P.S. I can't remember if I gave you the phone #(***) ***-**** of Mr. George the book author and friend of mine. Call or write > up to you girl!!

P.S. Almost forgot! Here is a visiting form for you to fill out and return to me. This way, if I can ever get you out here, you'll already be approved to "come on in"!! Can't tell no lies on the form. (Smile!)

Love Ya! Love Ya!

Featherwood :   11/12/98

        Hello! At just now, a very few minutes ago, received your letter & (2) "religious tracts" dated 11/4/98! As always, I was very pleased to hear from you because your my little buddy! I'm of the opinion that you are under the impression on a couple of matters that are in error. I want these very small "differences" or "misunderstandings" (nice sized word, huh? Smile!) cleared up now!

        Lee Ann, I don't think you are "dumping" on me. I don't know how or why you think your "dumping" on me. It simply isn't true that I think like that! Period! That's straight out ██ — ██! Featherwood, you are my friend! I care about "my friends" a whole lot. But, I tell you true, your becoming more than a friend to me; your becoming like a daughter to me! My favorite part of this last letter you write me, (wrote me, yeah, I missed that one!) is what your brother did for you on that "prom dress" regardless of when the prom happens!

(OVER)

I'd like to shake his hand and give him a big ol hug!! That's just great what that kid did, ~~especially~~ for his baby sister!! Please tell him I send him my regards and respect. I truly enjoyed coming to that part in your letter. To me, that is indeed an act of love!!

    I had hoped that you would have received my present to you also. Since you didn't mention it, I'm assuming that you never received it. The man who wrote this last "Manson book", Ed George, is a personal friend of mine. He worked for the California Department of Corrections for (32) years before he retired a few years ago. I worked as his clerk for (5) or (6) years and we truly became "friends" but we both knew there was a "line" that neither one of us ever crossed. Since his retirement, we went through all the proper rules + regulations and now he comes to visit with me every (3) or (4) months. He can't afford more because I eat up about $20.00 worth of food and soda water every time we visit! Hah!

the book   I helped him a lot in writing pictures, and I gave him a lot of at $2.00 apiece, which I paid for, that are in the book. Although it

(2.)

is primarely about Charlie, he does write about others, me included, and himself. I knew you went looking for it, I believe you even went to Jackson, Tennessee, didn't you? And you couldn't find it. So, I wrote him and requested that he autograph it and mail you a copy in time for your birthday. I wanted you to read it and let your folks read it. Then, I wanted to let you know how me & Charlie could sign it for you. With the pictures & the (3) autographs, you would have your car and a nice one at that! (Smile!) Now I've got to write and ask him what happened. Hopefully it will be done when he gets my letter in the next couple days. Rest assured of this, I flat-out promise you'll get the book exactly how I told you! Period!!

Now, you'll know what happened with the other "Tennessee Girl" as I've had that sent for a few days now. In fact, I've been awaiting your response on that particular letter with anticipation. So, hope you're already

③ (OVER)

written that letter before you even get this letter from me. (Smile!) It was a truly sad time for me because that kid was an amazing young woman. LeAnn, I sure wish you'd put her on your "prayer list". It is amazing how much her death affected me considering all the mayhem & murder she seen and even, to my eternal shame, become involved in them personally. Yes, I know that I'm "born again" in Christ Jesus, and am a "new" man! And Praise God for that! Thank you Jesus!! But, I also know that I'll never "forget" what I've done in this life.

Oh yeah! Back to "dumping" for a couple of minutes. If you have any problems or whatever it may be, and you need someone to share them with, I'm here for you. Anytime — anything! (I will put one "qualifier" on that. In deference to our ages & gender, I'm an "ol' fogee" on "sexual matters" and would not like to hear them from you or any other young lady — unless — there absolutely is no one else to go to that you believe will give you help. Then, come to me because I will help you out of anything I possibly can! That's a promise from me to you — and it won't EVER change in any way, shape or form. Okay? O.K.!

④

⑤.   To answer some questions you asked
I'll go right down the line, okay? Here it is:
① It's going sadly slow but we will make it! (Smile.)
② Yes, me + Charlie are still in "the hole". It's
been a couple of days off of (60) days now. And,
we truly didn't do nothing wrong - speaking
for myself!
③ Featherwood, you don't have to apologize
to me on the doggone envelopes! If you
get some and don't care about them, cool!
Send them! As for other things, don't worry
a bit, I'll not ask because I know things
are tough for a young person. Also, I can't
call you while I'm in "the hole". Maybe I
can work something out when I do get out.
But, I cannot call any way except the so-
called "collect" way!! That isn't my fault.
And I can't change it! I would if I could!!
④ I never for one moment didn't think
you went to "boot camp". Seriously, I
didn't. Yes, I knew you didn't go to
Georgia but I didn't care about it
all that much. If you truly didn't
want to continue to write me -
that's your choice - either way!
⑤ I keep telling you that your a young
(OVER)

lady and your going to change your mind about a lot of things until you mature. That's your privilege. That process is yours to do — we all go through that. And it is our honor & duty as mature adults to be there with you whenever you need us. That's what "love" is all about. Don't trip on this too much. Your not doing anything wrong at all!! Okay? OK!!

5. Here is another one from my Mexican friend Eddie. He, too, is a Christian even though he hasn't been "born again" he is definitely headed that way if I have anything to do with it!! (Smile!) (Big Smile!) I told him about your having written me some poems (I saved them but I can't have all my property in the "hole" so they are in my property) so he told me I could give you some of his stuff. Will do so every time I get a chance, okay!! OK!!

6. Maybe you'll send us some — okay?

(II)

(e) I'll give Charlie your "Happy Birthday" wish. I'm sure he returns them to you. Also, yes, we both know your not selling stuff we sent you. But, even if you did, I don't think it would bother us a bit. Once you've been given something, it is yours to do with as you like. It's yours!!.

(f) Last thing. Your letter is dated 11/4/98 by you. It is postmarked 11/4/98 in Jackson, Tennessee. I got it this date 11/12/98 — so it must have taken (8) days to reach me. Not bad considering at least one weekend, (2) days, and the (1) holiday (11/11/98).

Gotta go girl! I'm here for you. Our Lord & Savior did indeed "bless me" with bringing you into my life. Thank you Jesus!!
Love, Roger Dale*

He + You are both
My Friends!!
—————— 11/12/98 ——————

P.S.S. I can't remember if I
gave you the phone # (██) ██-██
of Mr. George the book author and
friend of mine.   Mr. Ed. George
                              ███ ██ ███ █,
Call or write   ██████ ██ ██,
        Up to you girl!!   █████
                  ⟶ 86/21/11 ——————

P.S. almost forgot! Here is a visiting
form for you to fill out and return
to me. This way, if I can ever
get you out here, you'll already
be approved to "come on in"!!
Can't tell no lies on the form.
Love YA!   Smile!   Love Ya!

"No longer will they teach their neighbor, or say to one another, 'Know the Lord,' because they will all know me, from the least of them to the greatest," declares the Lord. "For I will forgive their wickedness and will remember their sins no more."

(Jeremiah 31:34 NIV)

Jesus paid a tremendous price for us so we could have abundant life. He willingly took all of our sin on Himself and gave His life on the cross so we could be forgiven and have new life in Him.

(Joyce Meyer)

LETTER 14

Roger Dale Smith
A-93198-C   4A-4R-20-L
P.O. Box 3476 (Ad. Seg.)
Corcoran, California 93212-3476

STATE
PRISON
CORCORAN

Le Ann Redding

█████ █████ █████

Lexington, Tennessee
38351

USA 32

38351/1636

11/12/98

"Featherwood":

This is a picture of my grandmother and grandfather taken in 1963 or 1964. <u>Please</u> return it to me. It is priceless to me. Wish I had copies but I don't. These are the ones I lived with from shortly after my birth until I was (6) years old. I love them both more than anyone on this planet!! I'm looking forward to being able to give them <u>BIG</u> kisses & hugs when I get there with Christ our Savior & Redeemer. Glory! They both lived all their lives and are now buried within (20) miles of where you are at. If I knew exactly where I'd tell you so you could go to their graves and pray that both of them found their "new home" with God Almighty is a 1,000,000,000,000,000,000,000,000- (1) <u>decillion times</u> better than all the homes they ever knew. I am looking forward to introducing you to them when you get there! (Smile!) <u>If</u> you'd call my mother and tell her to write me because I don't have her address or give it to you to give to me, I would really appreciate it!! Also, tell her to send me some pictures of her when she was young- Why? Because I don't have any of her but the S.Q. ones!

Gotta Go!
Me

"Heatherwood":   11/12/98

       This is a picture of my grand-
mother and grandfather taken in 1963 or
1964. Please return it to me. It is priceless
to me. Wish I had copies but I don't. These
are the ones I lived with from shortly after
my birth until I was (6) years old. I love
them both more than anyone on this planet!! I'm
looking forward to being able to give them BIG
kisses & hugs when I get there with Christ our
Savior & Redeemer. Glory! They both lived all
their lives and are now buried within (20) miles
of where you are at. If I knew exactly where
                                    (OVER)

I'd tell you so you could go to their graves and pray that both of them found their "new home" with God almighty is a 1,000,000, 000,000, 000, 000, 000, 000 —(1) decillion times is better than all the homes they ever knew. I am looking forward to introducing you to them when you get there! (Smile!) If you'd call my mother and tell her to write me because I don't have her address or give it to you to give to me, I would really appreciate it! Also, tell her to send me some pictures of her when she was young. Why? Because I don't have any of her but the S.Q. ones!

go to over

The Son is the radiance of God's glory and the exact representation of his being, sustaining all things by his powerful word. After he had provided purification for sins, he sat down at the right hand of the Majesty in heaven.

(Hebrews 1:3 NIV)

There are no sins unpardonable today … there is no forgiveness of sin on the other side of this life.

(Dr. Charles Stanley)

LETTER 15

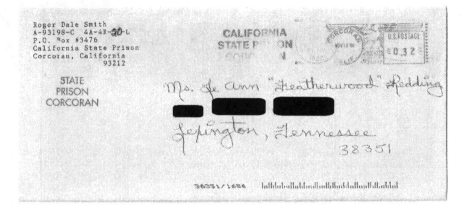

Roger Dale Smith
A-93198-C   4A-4R-30-L
P.O. Box #3476
California State Prison
Corcoran, California
            93212

STATE
PRISON
CORCORAN

CALIFORNIA
STATE PRISON

U.S.POSTAGE
$0.32

Ms. Le Ann "Featherwood" Redding

Lexington, Tennessee
                    38351

38351/1638   luldulubudlabluullubldludubulbudltllubludbul

11/16/98

"Featherwood":

Hello, "Tennessee Girl", just a few short lines to say hi and make a couple of remarks!! (Smile!) By now I'm hoping that you wrote because I'd like to know <u>if</u> you received that book, "Taming The Beast", from Mr. Ed George as your birthday gift from me? I certainly hope so because I gave him a lot of help in the writing of the book and he & me are supposed to be friends. I simply didn't have the money ($25.00) to buy it myself so I asked him to do it for me. I pointed out that your just a young girl and that there never has & nor ever will be any relationship between us other than "friends" or maybe even "brother-sister" or "father-daughter." As such, it's kind of a really good feeling to be there for you and every once in awhile, be able to give you something that you'd really like to have- like this book trip <u>if</u> he did as I asked him to do for me. <u>If</u> he didn't do it by now, 11/15/98, I'm going to be a little mad at him. It pleases me very much to be able to do even little bitty things for you. I've never fathered a child but I've <u>always</u> had a very, very good relationship with children from infancy to young adulthood.

I'm sending you a "collectors" ad run by "Sothby's Auction House." As you can see Charlie's "stuff" sells for (<u>5</u>) to (<u>6</u>) <u>times</u> that "Dean Martin/Jerry Lewis", "Madona", "Earth, Wind & Fire" and others sell for. A simple poem or song is going for well over a thousand dollars!! Don't ask me why this is so because I truly can't figure it out- but I'm happy it is so because I'd like to get you that car you wanted your dad to get you. I'm not saying that I positively can do it, but <u>I am</u> <u>telling</u> <u>you</u> that I'll do everything in my power to get you a nice car or pick-up truck as a gift from your real daddy because, ever since you told me about that I've just got this feeling that your daddy would do almost anything to get his baby girl a gift like that! And because I somehow "know his heart" in regards to this one thing! It's something I'd like to help that man to do for his baby girl! We shall see. Okay, that's it for now LeAnn!! I'm way ahead of you on letters!! Pray for me. I always pray for you. Gone for now!!

R.D. Smith

11/16/98

"Featherwood":

        Hello, "Tennessee Girl",
just a few short lines to say hi and
make a couple of remarks!! (Smile!)
By now I'm hoping that you wrote because I'd like to know if you received
that book, "Taming The Beast", from Mr.
Ed George as your birthday gift from
me? I certainly hope so because I
gave him a lot of help in the writing
of the book and he & me are supposed to be friends. I simply didn't have
the money ($25.00) to buy it myself my-
self so I asked him to do it for
me. I pointed out that your just a
young girl and that there never has &
nor ever will be any relationship between us other than "friends" or maybe even "brother-sister" or "father-daugh-
ter". As such, it's kind of a really
good feeling to be there for you and
every once in awhile, be able to give
you something that you'd really like
to have — like this book trip if he
did as I asked him to do for me.

If he didn't do it by now, 11/15/98, I'm going to be a little mad at him. It pleases me very much to be able to do even little bitty things for you. I've never fathered a child but I've always had a very, very good relationship with children from ~~infancy~~ to young adulthood.

I'm sending you a "collectors" ad run by "Sotheby's Auction House". As you can see Charlie's "stuff" sells for (5) to (8) times that "Dean Martin / Jerry Lewis", "Madona", "Earth, Wind & Fire" and others sell for. A simple poem or song is going for well over a thousand dollars!! Don't ask me why this is so because I truly can't figure it out — but I'm happy it is so because I'd like to get you that car you wanted your dad to get you. I'm not saying that I positively can do it, but I am telling you that I'll do everything in my power to get you a nice car or pick-up truck as a gift from your real daddy because, ever since you told me about that I've just got this feeling that your daddy would do almost anything to get his baby girl a gift like that! And because I somehow "know his heart" in regards to this one thing! It's something I'd like to help that man to do for his baby girl!! We shall see - Okay, that's it for now Jo*Ann!! I'm way ahead of you on letters !! Pray for me, I always pray for you- Gone for now! R. D. Smith ✱

②

Everything and everyone that the Father has given me will come to me, and I won't turn any of them away.

(John 6:37 CEV)

Christ is a substitute for everything, but nothing is a substitute for Christ.

(Harry Ironside)

LETTER 16

Roger Dale Smith
A-93198-C   4A-4R-20-L
P.O. Box 3476 (Ad. Seg.)
Corcoran, California 93212-3476

Ms. Le Ann "Heatherwood "Redding

Lexington

11/16/98

Featherwood!

Hello girl! Just thought I'd write and say hello!

Don't have a lot to say. Just kind of cruising along and thinking of our Lord & Savior Christ Jesus! LeAnn, keep me on "your prayer list" as I keep you & yours on mine! The fervent prayers of a few righteous people availith much! Praise God!! We <u>do</u> have a living, loving, merciful, kind father & God!! Let's just set a date and time and we, you & I, will go into our private prayer closet and pray, okay? How about December 1, 1998? At exactly 9:00 P.M. your time? Is this cool with you?

Here are the latest drawings my friend drew. Also, that "Sothby's" the "English Auction House" has set their appraised of famous and infamous Americans. You guessed it!- Charlie was #1! Weird, huh?

Your friend- always!
Your friend- forever!
—Me

11/16/98

Featherwood!

Hello girl! Just thought
I'd write and say hello!

Don't have a lot to say.
Just kind of cruising along and
thinking of our Lord & Savior
Christ Jesus! Jo Ann, keep me
on "your prayer list" as I
keep you & yours on mine!
The fervent prayers of a few
righteous people availeth much!
Praise God!! We do have a living,
loving, merciful, kind father & God!!
Let's just set a date and time
and we, you & I, will go into
our private prayer closet and
pray, okay? How about December
1, 1998? At exactly 9:00 P.M. your
time? Is this cool with you?
Here are the latest draw-
ings my friend drew. Also, that
"Sotheby's" the "English Auction House"
has set their appraised of famous
and infamous Americans. You guessed
it! — Charlie was #1! Weird, huh?

Your friend — always!
Your brother — forever!
                              — ME ✳

— Le Ann —
"Featherwood"
— Redding —

My
Lil
Bud!

Love
In
Jesus.

God Bless
+
Keep You
+
Yours!
Forever!

For I am convinced that neither death nor life, neither angels nor demons, neither the present nor the future, nor any powers, neither height nor depth, nor anything else in all creation, will be able to separate us from the love of God that is in Christ Jesus our Lord.

(Romans 8:38–39 NIV)

Have you ever thought you finally did the one thing that was bad enough that God will not forgive you? There is no such thing. There is nothing you can do; there is nothing someone else can do; there is nothing that the world, or the devil, or anything else in all of creation can do to separate you from the love that God has given you.

(52 Bible Verses You Should Have on Your Heart)

LETTER 17

Roger Dale Smith
A-93198-C   4A-4R-20-L   CALIFORNIA
P.O. Box # 3476 (Ad. Seg.)   STATE PRISON
Corcoran, California 93212-3476

        STATE
        PRISON
        CORCORAN

                        Le Ann "Featherwood" Redding

                        ▂▂▂ ▂▂▂▂ ▂▂▂▂▂

                        Lexington, Tennessee
                                              38351

"Featherwood"
God has not promised
skies always blue,
Flower-strewn pathways
all our lives through.
God hath not promised
sun without rain,
Joy without sorrow
peace without pain.
But God hath promised
strength for the day,
Rest for the labor,
light for the way.
Grace for the trials,
Help from above,
Unfailing sympathy,
undying love.
"Jesus is Lord"

Much Love,
Roger Dale

" Featherwood "

God has not promised
  skies always blue,
Flower – strewn pathways
  all our life's through;
God hath not promised
  sun without rain,
Joy without sorrow
  peace without pain.

But God hath promised
  strength for the day,
Rest for the labor,
  light for the way.
Grace for the trials,
  help from above,
Unfailing sympathy,
  undying love.

"Jesus is Lord"

Much Love,
Roger Dale

But whoever is united with the Lord is one with him in spirit ...

(1 Corinthians 6:17 NIV)

Through salvation our past has been forgiven, our present is given meaning, and our future is secured.

(Rick Warren)

LETTER 18

Roger Dale Smith
A-93198-C   4A-4A-20-L
P.O. Box # 3476 (Ad. Seg.)
Corcoran, California 93212-3476

Ms. Le Ann "Heatherwood" Redding

Lexington, Tennessee
38351

12/12/98

Featherwood:

Here is your approval to visit with me! So, whenever it becomes possible, you are approved to come and visit with me! That is really cool! (Smile!)

LeAnn, please call my mom and get her address for me, okay? I don't have her address and I'd like to write her <u>before</u> Christmas.

This is just a note. I'll write more later on. "Featherwood", please keep me in your prayers. I really need prayer in my life. I'll write more later.

With much love,
Roger Dale

12/12/98

Featherwood :

    Here is your approval to visit with me! So, whenever it becomes possible, you are approved to come and visit with me! That is really cool! (Smile!)

    Je Ann, please call my mom and get her address for me, okay? I don't have her address and I'd like to write her before Christmas.

    This is just a note. I'll write more later on. "Featherwood", please keep me in your prayers. I really need prayer in my life. I'll write more later.

With much love,

Roger Dale

STATE OF CALIFORNIA   DEPARTMENT OF CORRECTIONS
CDC 887   INMATE COPY

NOTICE OF VISITOR
APPROVAL/DENIAL/TERMINATION/SUSPENSION

INMATE'S NAME   CDC NUMBER HOUSING
TO: SMITH, ROGER D   A93198   4A4R00000000 20L
RE: REDDING, LEANN D

THE PERSON IDENTIFIED ABOVE HAS REQUESTED APPROVAL TO VISIT WITH YOU.

HIS/HER REQUEST HAS BEEN APPROVED.

IT IS YOUR RESPONSIBILITY TO INFORM YOUR VISITOR.

VISITORS MAY APPEAL ANY ACTION TAKEN ABOVE BY WRITING A LETTER TO THE WARDEN
OF THIS INSTITUTION.

But when this priest had offered for all time one sacrifice for sins, he sat down at the right hand of God, and since that time he waits for his enemies to be made his footstool. For by one sacrifice he has made perfect forever those who are being made holy.

(Hebrews 10:12–14 NIV)

The individual who desires to have his sins forgiven, must seek for it through the blood of Jesus. The individual who desires to get power over sin, must likewise seek it through the blood of Jesus.

(George Muller)

LETTER 19

Roger Dale Smith
A-93198-C   4A-4R-20-L
P.O. Box 3476 (Ad. Seg.)
Corcoran, California 93212-3476

STATE
PRISON
CORCORAN

Ms. Le ann Featherwood Redding

Lexington, Tonnessee

12/21/98

"Featherwood"

Have a very nice & safe Christmas day! May our Lord & Savior Jesus Christ know that we, you & I, truly celebrate His birth & death on this planet.

As you suggested, I'll be praying on Christmas day with you at 9:00 a.m. my time- 12:00 noon your time. All my love is Christ Jesus and you on this special day! I will check on your book- promise!!

Roger Dale

"Heatherwood"

Have a very nice & safe Christmas day! May our Lord & Savior Jesus Christ know that we, you & I, truly celebrate His birth & death on this planet. As you suggested, I'll be praying on Christmas day with you at 9:00 A.M. my time - 12:00 Noon your time. All my love is Christ Jesus and you on this special day! I will check on your book - promise !!

Roger Dale

NO: A-93198   NAME: SMITH, ROGER   4A4R-20L   CDC-128G
CUSTODY: MAX BS   WGPG: D1D   CS :373   ACTION: 30 DAY A/S REVIEW. RETAIN A/S
MEPD: 10-30-77   MERD: N/A   RC:12-2-98 PENDING O/C OF SSU INVESTIGATION. RET
AFFIL: N/A   ETH: WHI   SC/WA YARD.

COMMENTS:I/M SMITH made a personal appearance before FAC IV-A ICC this date for the purpose of a 30 Day Ad/Seg Review. "S" stated that he was in good health and ready to proceed. Comm elected to retain A/S pending the outcome of the SSU investigation regarding illegal business at activity with I/M Mason CDC # B-33920. Comm elected to retain S/C W/A yard. "S" stated that he understood the Comm's action, and inquired as to the excepted length of the investigation. The ICC Chairman stated that when we know something definitive that "S" would be brought back to ICC as soon as possible. Mr. Smith told the Psych Tech, S. Mason, that he was having serious Psychiatric problems. He further stated that he does not want to be housed in PHU. "S" request from removal from PHU will be re-evaluated once the A/S investigation is completed. Appeal rights and Shooting Policy were explained. No further Classification issues were addressed this date.

VN: vr cc: I/M

J. MARSHALL   R. COMFORT   S. MASON   V. NELSON
CHAIRPERSON/CDW(A)   FAC.CAPT(A)   MEMBER/LCSW   RECORDER/CCI
DATE: 10-28-98   FAC IV A   ICC   CLASSIFICATION   CSP-CORCORAN

Blessed is the one whose transgressions are forgiven, whose sins are covered. Blessed is the one whose sin the Lord does not count against them and in whose spirit is no deceit.

(Psalm 32:1–2 NIV)

To Forgive:

1 to cease to feel resentment against (an offender): to forgive one's enemies

2 to give up resentment of or claim to requital: forgive an insult

3 to grant relief from payment: forgive a debt

Intransitive Verb: to grant forgiveness: had to learn to forgive and forget

(Merriam-Webster 2019)

LETTER 20

Roger Dale Smith
A-93198-C   4A-4R-20-L
P.O. Box #3476
California State Prison - Corcoran
Corcoran, California 93212

CALIFORNIA
STATE PRISON
CORCORAN

CORCORAN
CALIF
U.S.POSTAGE
$ 0 33

STATE
PRISON
CORCORAN

Le Ann Redding

Lexington, Tenn.
38351

1/11/99

Featherwood:

Hello! I got your Christmas card and the camera & gum were confiscated by the prison officials. Here is the receipt they sent me. LeAnn, I thought I'd explained the prison rules about what we prisoners can and cannot have sent to us in here. Maybe I didn't. Other than stamps, when we are not in "the hole", you pretty much can't send me anything but "embossed" envelopes, (when we are on "Ad. Seg." status) stamps, (when we aren't in "the hole") and money orders. Not a lot, huh? Anything you may want to send- don't!! Ask me first if you can send something, okay? Okay!! Do you want me to send this camera & gum back to you or donate it to charity? Please tell me.

Also, I think I'm being transferred to another prison within a week or two. Maybe back to the one I was stabbed in back in March of 1998. I'll let you know my new address as soon as I get there.

Also, "Featherwood", will you please call my mom and tell her to send me her current address? I can't call her and I can't write her because I don't have her current address. I want to write her but can't because I lost/misplaced her address. In case you don't have it, she is staying with my sister and her phone # is (***) ***-****. Either tell her to write me so I can write her or get her address and send it to me in your next letter, okay? I like writing her because she may not be here too much longer and I want to make absolutely sure that she & me are on the best of terms before that day comes. LeAnn, please do this for me, okay? Okay!!

Also, you write pretty good letters on that word processor! Maybe you could write a couple of letters for me to send to all the TV stations, radio stations & newspapers to draw some attention to the fact that me & Charlie are still locked-up and still haven't received any kind of "write-up" on disciplinary charges even though it will soon be (6) months since we got locked-up!! I personally am beginning to believe it is a "conspiracy" to do us some harm and I'm debating whether to flood the local media with letters telling them what is going on over here! The bad thing is that I don't believe in taking my complaints to the "free world" for resolution. I'd prefer to settle them "in-house" if at all possible. Think you could do me a good job and type out my letter on your computer/word processor? Let me know girl! Will write more later. Take care & keep me in your prayers as I do you and yours. I love you Featherwood!!

Roger Dale

1/11/99

Featherwood:

Hello! I got your Christmas card and the camera & gum were confiscated by the prison officials. Here is the receipt they sent me. Jo Ann, I thought I'd explained the prison rules about what we prisoners can and cannot have sent to us in here. Maybe I didn't. Other than stamps, when we are not in "the hole", you pretty much can't send me anything but "embossed" envelopes, (when we are on "Ad. Seg." status) stamps, (when we aren't in "the hole") and money orders. Not a heck of a lot, huh? Anything you may want to send — don't!! ask me first if you can send something, okay? Okay. Do you want me to send this camera & gum back to you or donate it to charity? Please tell me.

Also, I ~~think~~ I'm being trans- ferred to another prison within a week or two. Maybe back to the one I was stabbed in back in March of 1998. I'll let you know my new address as soon as I get there.

Also, "Featherwood", will you please call my mom and tell her to send me her current address? I can't call her and I can't write her because I don't have her current address. I want to write her but

(OVER)

(2) can't because I lost/misplaced her address.
In case you don't have it, she is staying with
my sister and her phone # is: (■) ■-■■■■.
Either tell her to write me so I can write her or
get her address and send it to me in your next
letter, okay? I like writing her because she may
not be here too much longer and I want to
make absolutely sure that she & me are on
the best of terms before that day comes. Le—
Ann please do this for me, okay? Okay!!

              Also, you write pretty good letters on
that word processor! Maybe you could write a
couple of letters for me to send to all the TV
stations, radio stations & newspapers to draw
some attention to the fact that me & Charlie are
still locked-up and still haven't received any
kind of "write-up" on disciplinary charges even
though it will soon be (6) months since we
got locked-up!! I personally am beginning
to believe it is a "conspiracy" to do us some
harm and am debating whether to flood the
local media with letters telling them what is
going on over here! The bad thing is that
I don't believe in taking my complaints
to the "free world" for resolution. I'd prefer
to settle them "in-house" if at all possible.
Think you could do me a good job and type
out my letter on your computer/word processor?
Let me know girl! Will write more later. Take
care & keep me in your prayers as I do you
and yours. I Love You Featherwood!! Roger
                                              Dale

NOTIFICATION OF DISAPPROVAL - MAIL/PACKAGES/PUBLICATIONS

INMATE'S NAME	CDC NUMBER
R. D. Smith	A.931982 - 4H4R-20L

MAIL / PACKAGES SECTION (Complete for mail or package cases only)

☒ INCOMING MAIL/PACKAGE ☐ OUTGOING MAIL/PACKAGE

LIST ITEM(S) WHICH MEET DISAPPROVAL CRITERIA
1 small camera & 5 pkgs of film

DESCRIPTION OF MATERIAL THAT MEETS DISAPPROVAL CRITERIA, INCLUDE CCR, TITLE 15 SECTION
cameras are not allowed.

DISPOSITION	SENDER INFORMATION		
	FIRST NAME	MI	LAST NAME
☐ HELD PENDING INVESTIGATION/APPEAL	E.	Wood	
☐ RETURNED TO SENDER _____ (Date)	ADDRESS (NUMBER AND STREET) 230 White St		
☐ DESTROYED	CITY Lexington	STATE TN	ZIP CODE 38351
*(INMATE HAS FIFTEEN (15) DAYS, AFTER NOTIFICATION OF DISAPPROVAL HAS BEEN FORWARDED, TO LET STAFF KNOW THE CHOICE OF DISPOSAL, OTHERWISE MATERIAL WILL BE DESTROYED).	I ACKNOWLEDGE RECEIPT OF THIS NOTIFICATION: (INMATE'S SIGNATURE)		DATE SIGNED

AUTHORITY TO DISALLOW (Must be completed in all cases)

PRINTED NAME OF WARDEN'S DESIGNEE	SIGNATURE OF WARDEN'S DESIGNEE	DATE SIGNED	DATE FORWARDED TO INMATE
Jester		10-29-98	

PUBLICATIONS SECTION (Complete for publication cases only)

TITLE OF PUBLICATION (Include issue/date)	PUBLISHER	PAGE(S) WHICH MEET DISAPPROVAL CRITERIA

DESCRIPTION OF MATERIAL THAT MEETS DISAPPROVAL CRITERIA, INCLUDE CCR, TITLE 15 SECTION

DISPOSITION	DESIGNEE INFORMATION		
	FIRST NAME	MI	LAST NAME
☐ HELD PENDING INVESTIGATION/APPEAL			
☐ DESTROYED	ADDRESS (NUMBER AND STREET)		
☐ RETURNED TO OUTSIDE DESIGNEE AT INMATE'S EXPENSE _____ (Date)	CITY	STATE	ZIP CODE
**(INMATE HAS FIFTEEN (15) DAYS, AFTER NOTIFICATION OF DISAPPROVAL HAS BEEN FORWARDED, TO LET STAFF KNOW THE CHOICE OF DISPOSAL, OTHERWISE MATERIAL WILL BE DESTROYED).	I ACKNOWLEDGE RECEIPT OF THIS NOTIFICATION: (INMATE'S SIGNATURE)		DATE SIGNED

AUTHORITY TO DISALLOW (Must be completed in all cases)

FACILITY CAPTAIN'S PRINTED NAME	FACILITY CAPTAIN'S SIGNATURE	DATE SIGNED	DATE FORWARDED TO INMATE

For if you forgive other people when they sin against you, your heavenly Father will also forgive you. But if you do not forgive others their sins, your Father will not forgive your sins.

(Matthew 6:14–15 NIV)

I believe that Christians believe in salvation by grace through faith in Jesus Christ, not by works. And we believe that if you're saved, Jesus becomes your savior. He makes a promise to you. You can trust his promises. You can bank on that word.

(Robert H. Schuller)

LETTER 21

USA H
First Class Rate

Le Ann "Featherwood" Redding

STATE
PRISON
CORCORAN

Lexington, Tennessee

38351

Roger Dale Smith
A-93198-C   4A-4R-50-L
P.O. Box # 3476
Corcoran, California
93212
4

...I'LL SCREAM!

FROM *Roger Dale*

"*Jesus is Lord*"

Very truly I tell you, whoever hears my word and believes him who sent me has eternal life and will not be judged but has crossed over from death to life.

(John 5:24 NIV)

Repenting and coming unto Christ through the covenants and ordinances of salvation are prerequisite to and a preparation for being sanctified by the reception of the Holy Ghost and standing spotless before God at the last day.

(David A. Bednar)

LETTER 22

BAKE... 6 FEB

Le Ann "Featherwood" Redding

STATE
PRISON
CORCORAN *Arlington, Tennessee*

38351

Charles M. Manson
#B-33920 4A-4R-48-L
P.O. Box #3476
Corcoran, California
93212

...HOPE YOU GET
LOTS OF "UGHS
AND SQUISHES"!

FROM

I have swept away your sins like a cloud. I have scattered your offenses like the morning mist. Oh, return to me, for I have paid the price to set you free.

(Isaiah 44:22 NLT)

Jesus is our high priest. He is at the right hand of God on our behalf, and yet He knows everything that we are going through. He understands the weakness of being human. He understands pain, suffering, and temptation, and yet He lived a perfect life. He shows the power of God through the weakness of humanity. We know that we can go before God open, vulnerable, and without fear, because Christ has gone before us and made the atonement for our sin.

(52 Bible Verses You Should Have on Your Heart)

LETTER 23

Roger Dale Smith
A-93198-C 4A-4R-50-R
P.O. Box #3476 (P.H.U.)
Corcoran, California
                    93212

STATE
PRISON
CORCORAN

Ms. LeAnn "Featherwood" Redding
Lexington, Tennessee   38351

38351+1656

10-26-99

LeAnn,

Hello "Featherwood"! Or maybe you have become a young woman and no longer like that name(?) It happens. Most so-called "nicknames" are loved and cherished by young kids but they become "boring" to older people. However, as I told you before, in prison, which is all I truly know, for a "good wood", ("Peckerwood") usually a young white Southern boy, being called a "Peckerwood" or "Good Wood" is considered a big "honor" or compliment. And, as with all other things, quite naturally, these type of people, like me, pass the "honor" or compliment along when we run across a "good white girl". We call them "Featherwood". Be that as it may, both you & I have a higher calling; we both are believers in, and followers of, Christ Jesus! Praise His Most Holy Name! Glory!!

I've now known you for (3) years and I truly cherish your friendship. Your very simply a beautiful person; inside and out. Your beauty is in your smile & in your heart. You absolutely "radiate" love, compassion & understanding. That is very rare at any age- but especially rare in one so young. It is very simply a pleasure to know you. LeAnn, your mom and dad did an excellant job of raising you. It is easy to see that they instilled in you a sense of morality and compassion. Even if you, at (15) years old, did want to contact Charlie and get a letter from him, you had no way of knowing just how your #1 "contact" with people like Charlie & I might turn out. Nor did you have any way of knowing that Charlie was illiterate and can barely read or write. Nor did you have any idea that a native Tennesseean, me, would be that first one to respond to your letter. Nor could either of us know that we would both be "Homies" living in Lexington, Tennessee! (Smile!)

But, your "first contact" (Smile!) letter was very, very well crafted and extremely well written by a (15) years old kid!! There simply was no choice for me. I had to respond and, in time, after I had set certain conditions, Charlie, too, has come to like you a lot. I have come to love you a whole lot. You, my young friend, are like my own child, which I've never had, and my younger sisters, which I do have!! Though all of them are now in their (30's)! Even more importantly, you are, like me, a "true" "child of God". Though all humans are God's "children", only the ones whom make a deliberate decision or "choice" to acknowledge him as both our "Father" and our "God"/"Lord" are His "true children." It is our "choice" to make and both of us have sincerely & truly made our choice-and- because of this one decision, the most important "decision" or "choice" any human being can ever make, we share a "bond" ("Followers of Christ") ("Christians") that can never be broken!! We, my beautiful young sister will soon be spending an eternity with our Lord & Savior Christ Jesus!! And though we don't truly comprehend or appreciate just how long an "eternity" is, we human beings having a so-called "finite" mind, once we are called "home" (Heaven), we will in addition to our "glorifided bodies" have an "infinite" mind and will then know what an "eternity" in the presence of our "Heavenly Father's" love, mercy, & grace truly means!! Glory to God Almighty & thank you Jesus!!

When we are young, we often think we are "invulnerable" and "impervious" to "Death." It truly very seldom enters our minds, as individuals or collectively in a group, that we might "die." "Death" is something which happens to "old people" or maybe "sick people" but not to young, healthy kids entering into the prime of our life. Then, on "Prom Night" or maybe just (4) or (5) of us "hanging-out" with our so-called "friends"- well- maybe we drink a few beers too many. Maybe we even sip a taste of "shine" or maybe we do a couple of "joints" or "doobies". Maybe even a combination of all three. I mean, hey!, we are young and we are just trying to have a little "fun". Man, Lexington is just a little "hick town" and other than Friday night football games, in season, there simply isn't a whole lot to do!! We just want to have a little "fun"!! That's all. But, on that very night, some man puts away a few too many at the local pub and, "accidently", even though we are smart and use the "designated driver" (usually the more responsible/mature friend amongst us) well, old "Bubba" doesn't give a hoot about all that "kid stuff". And a few days later, "Bubba" and all of us "friends" are laid to rest. Tragic? Yes, definitely! But, LeAnn "Featherwood" Redding, <u>you</u> are the "luckiest" one of all of us "friends". <u>You</u> knew Christ Jesus!! <u>You</u> accepted Him early on in your life and <u>you</u> will indeed have a new & glorious life, a life without end and without any sickness and death! <u>You</u> will, for all eternity, bask in the love & glory that only our Lord is able & ready to give to every single one of us that made the "decision/choice" to accept Him completely & with absolutely no reservations as both "Savior" <u>and</u> "Lord"!! Glory girl!! Glory!!

But, maybe our other (4) "friends" <u>didn't</u> make that "choice/decision" and no such "life" is in store for them. Maybe our Lord, in His infinite mercy, love & grace for each one of us poor human beings in our ignorance & defiance, regardless of age, color, or sexual gender, will display his compassion and those whom <u>didn't</u> make that one simple choice/decision will be granted that one so-called "second death" and simply cease to exist after "Judgement Day." We simply don't know what God will do. And, most Holy Father, maybe their futures will be so terrible & horrible in the "Pit" that it puts cold "goose bumps" all over my body! Afterall, we are told unequivocally that one poor soul in "Hell" begged God for just one single drop of water to lick off the rotted flesh on the finger of a "Leper". And God said simply: "No." And, when the former "rich man" that walked past that wasted, wretched, rotted "Leper" each day and never once stopped to give any assistance and/or help in any way, shape, fashion or form, saw that God was not moved by his begging, the poor man told God, "Well, Lord, I've got (5) brothers still living and none are "saved". Please, Lord, please let me tell them what has happened to me and cause them not to come where I am! Or, if that isn't even possible, will you, Lord, please see that they get my message?" And, our Lord said, "They, like you, have ears that will not hear and eyes that will not see." In all of God's Holy Word ("Holy Bible"), other that the things Christ Jesus bore for us, that one story is, to me, simply a "hideous" existence! There is no "life", no "love", no "mercy", no "grace", no "compassion" from our Lord. Even so, since He is "infallible" and cannot make a "mistake" or render an "unjust judgement", we, as "true children" of God, must accept the absolute reality of what took place with this poor wretched soul. He had a million, million opportunities to make his "choice/decision" but he chose not to accept Christ Jesus as Lord & Savior! Was he "stupid?" Well, despite the money and "social class" from whence he came, giving him the very best education & training possible, he deliberately chose to reject Christ Jesus (the Son) and God (the Father) and the Holy Spirit. So, yes indeed he was, and forever more will be, "stupid." But, given where he was then, is now, and will be forever more, being "stupid" is the very least of his troubles!!

No, his condition <u>does</u> <u>not</u> "please" me nor do I take any pleasure whatsoever in where he is at and in what horrible, hideous condition he will spend all eternity! Nor do I take this story "lightly". Just the reverse. I take it very seriously indeed. In fact, to be absolutely truthful and entirely candid with you, LeAnn, I am terrified, scared witless by this story!! You see, these other (5) souls were his "brothers" not simply his "friends", and they, too, would end up where he was, and all (6) of them, still are this very day- and <u>will</u> <u>be</u> forever & ever, "time without end"- for <u>all</u> "eternity!" As hideous as this knowledge is, and it is indeed the most horrible story I've read in the "Word" of God, accepting the "hideousness" that Jesus endured for <u>us</u>, it shows a personal side of God that <u>none</u> of us are "comfortable" with. Oh Yes! we are all "comfortable" with all of the "stories" of God's love, grace, mercy and compassion. They calm us and give us a feeling of "safety" & "secureness." And why is this? Because <u>we</u> made our "choice/decision" to accept, surrender & obey Christ Jesus!! And, because of this choice/decision we, <u>you</u> & <u>I</u>, made, <u>we</u> are "saved" from having to ever personally see this "side" of our God! And thank God for it!! You see, God truly is at "war" with "the enemy" (Satan) and though Christ Jesus has already <u>won</u> the victory and "saved" us, <u>if</u> we "choose" Him over (Satan) and defeated "Death" & "Sin", God, for reasons we don't know now, but will know when He calls us "Home", still allows (Satan) "the enemy" the time God promised him. But, LeAnn, <u>we</u>, <u>you</u> & <u>I</u>, don't have to "sweat it." We are, by the very blood & death of Christ Jesus, "healed" and "saved." Period! Praise Him, girl!

But, LeAnn, those "friends" of ours? And, yes, even the people we "dislike" (like poor old "Bubba") we <u>must</u> give "witness" to at each & every opportunity we have. This is not only our "duty" to Christ Jesus, it is also a <u>direct</u> <u>order</u> from God! There is nothing to "argue" about. No, being human, there are times we simply don't "feel like it". That is true. But, LeAnn, there is no doubt that Christ Jesus didn't "feel like" going through what He endured for <u>us</u>, <u>all</u> <u>of</u> <u>us</u>, <u>every</u> <u>single</u> <u>one</u> <u>of</u> <u>us</u>! In fact, He spent the entire night in that garden praying to His "true father" and asking that, if possible, "this cup be allowed to pass from me." But, in the end, because of His enormous love <u>and</u> respect for his one "true father", the same Father that He had spent time with out measure with through all the aeons, eons & ceaons of time with prior to his birth in human form, He simply bowed His majestic head and quietly said, "Thy Will Be Done." <u>Total</u> and absolute obedience to His Father <u>and</u> to our Father through Christ Jesus! <u>Glory</u>!

LeAnn, do you know what absolutely impressed me the most about Christ Jesus during His (33) years in the body of a man? Surprisingly, it <u>wasn't</u> the "miracles" He performed. It <u>wasn't</u> the pain & humiliation He endured just before & during His execution in a most heinous manner even though that was bad enough to make me "wince"- and cry!! When He begged for a single drink of water in His pain & misery on that Cross, some very sick & perverted "demon" in the guise of a Roman soldier had the absolute cruelty & viciousness to put a sponge full of "vinegar"- not water- on the end of his spear and press it to His bloodied & cracked lips to drink!! It was not even this cowardly & demonic act that gets me. But, again, I've <u>cried</u> about this one single, sadistic act many times. If you think about it, you will too!

LeAnn, Jesus <u>never</u> knew "sin". <u>Never</u>! God "hates", not "dislikes", "hates" sin so much that He cannot bear to see it. Think about it! God turns His face from "sin"!! Big or little "sins", to God, "sin is sin" and

He simply cannot tolerate it- period!! Can you imagine a newborn baby, in perfect health & perfect in body, mind & soul? The newborn is human and feels all that we feel. Fresh from the womb of a good mother where there was nothing "bad" to him/her as a fetus. No drugs, no alcohol, no tobacco products, no smog, no "bad" thing period. Conceived in love, carried (9) months in a "clean womb" with no disease and delivered quickly with no troubles, complications or discomfort. This newborn, innocent child is placed on a large round table made of solid cold metal with no "padding" or cloth of any kind. He/She starts to whimper in discomfort and gets very cold from the very cold steel table very fast. Around this very large round cold steel table are numerous sick, psychotic, truly evil people with some very, very, cold steel pliars, knives, scalpels, forks and numerous other instruments of torture & pain causing capability. And others have hot coals, blow-torches, molten lava, etc. (You get the idea.) They all start working, systematically, to deliver the utmost pain & injuries to this totally innocent newborn which has never once know pain & discomfort- but none-the-less feels every single grunion of the pain and screams & screams in pure and completely unadulterated pain & terror! Turns your stomach? Well it should. Mine, too! But this is simply an "illustration" as bad as it sounds and the sickness it conveys is only "illusionary". It never happened although the "Nazis" came close to it in W.W.11 at several of their "camps."

But, LeAnn, Jesus had <u>never</u> known "sin" <u>period</u>! And, like His Holy Father, He simply couldn't tolerate it in any manner- Period! (Not even a "little white lie" ("Fib"), stealing, rape or murder nor even "worship of Satan.") "Sin" is "Sin"- And <u>before</u> Christ Jesus- "the wages of "sin" are death." Period! And since every single human being but <u>Christ Jesus</u> that has ever lived, from "Adam & Eve" all the way up to 1999 with "Adam & Steve" has "sinned" thousands, if not millions of times, during our respective lifetimes, <u>before</u> Christ Jesus, there simply wasn't any "atonement" for what <u>we</u> <u>all</u> did and did very well indeed! It was and has always been within our very nature to "sin"- and in so doing- to incur the "Wrath of God" and suffer the death that our sins brought upon each and every single one of us!! Every single human being <u>but</u> Christ Jesus. In Him- there was no "sin"- Period!

But, LeAnn, at the very worst time in his short life in a human body ((33) years), beaten, whipped, scourged, spat upon, humiliated & finally nailed to a Cross, when He was at his weakest point in body, mind & spirit, crucified on that cross (Cross), He bore the "sins of the entire world"! Glory! Thank You Sweet Jesus!

Think of it! He whom had never known sin, could not in fact bear to see sin in any manner, shape or form- <u>every</u> single sin ever committed <u>before</u> His glorious birth in human form, during His short but all so glorious life span of only (33) years, and every single sin committed over the past nearly <u>2,000 years</u> and every single sin still to be committed until humanity as we know it comes to an end, was borne by that totally "newborn" on an old wooden rugged cross instead of a large round cold steel table! And LeAnn, Jesus also cried out in unspeakable & terribly hideous pain & terror- and even though He had been with God the Father for uncountable billions & trillions of years, time uncountable, aeons, eons, & oceans of time, and was "<u>One</u> <u>with</u> <u>the</u> <u>Father</u>" during all that time, He literally was so overwhelmed with that load of "sin", <u>our</u> <u>sin</u>, <u>yours</u> & <u>mine</u>, as well as every sin ever committed by every single human being who ever lived, is living now, and ever will live until "Judgement Day" when <u>all</u> humanity ceases to exist in the form we are now in, He got every sin ever committed laid on His body, mind & soul! And His absolute terror & agony was so great He screamed, "My God, hast thou forsaken me?" He didn't make a statement. He was in doubt. He asked a question! Have you any concept of the magnitude of his agony & terror & absolute, total helplessness that would make Him question whether or not His One & Only True Father would totally leave Him alone in his human and His "Godly" suffering?

It is absolutely inconceivable for Christ Jesus to question the one & only "God" with which He is "One With"? Then He "died" a human death. And, most glorious of all things, (3) days later He was resurrected by God the Father and "Sin" & "Death" were totally defeated for all time! Glory to the Father! Glory to the Son! Glory to the Holy Spirit! Glory!- "3 in 1" = <u>GOD</u>!!

Now, <u>that</u> impresses me! That stirs my blood! That, to me, is the true definition of exactly what "God the Father" meant when it was written in His Word, "For God so loved the world … ". (John 3:16 NIV) Is it any wonder I want to witness? Is it any wonder that I want to carry the "gospel" ("good news") to <u>anyone</u> who will listen? No, I simply am not capable of "repaying" my Lord & Savior Christ Jesus for <u>that</u> (what He suffered when that whole load of "Sin" came down on Him). And I can't "earn" my way into "Glory" because it can't be done. But, LeAnn, "Featherwood", <u>I</u> <u>cannot</u> tell a lie I usually tell. <u>I</u> <u>cannot</u> think an evil thought I used to love; <u>I</u> <u>cannot</u> do an "abomination" with some young & foolish "girly boy" whom I used to dearly love. In short, <u>I</u> <u>can</u> lessen that "load of sin" that my Glorious Lord & Savior Christ Jesus bore on that dark day by not doing even (1) stinking so-called "little sin" or "major sin" even though, to God, "sin is sin"- Period! And every "sin" <u>I</u> <u>don't</u> <u>do</u> lessens that load He carried that dark but glorious day! Thank You Lord Jesus! And every "sin" <u>you</u> don't do, does the same thing! And every "sin" that someone else <u>doesn't</u> <u>do</u> because we bore witness to them and revealed what God revealed to us, also lightens that awful load even more. <u>We</u>, you & I, <u>can</u> make a difference. We both <u>can</u> make a difference. We <u>both</u> can tell everyone we meet the "Good News", the absolutely wonderful news of the "Gospel of Jesus Christ". We <u>can</u> spread His love & mercy and grace! We <u>can</u>, as both God the Father & Christ Jesus the Son, <u>commands</u> us to do, not "asks" or "requests" us to do, but "orders" us to do, Love one another and surrender our hearts, bodies & souls to Christ Jesus and do His Will- not our own will!! And, <u>if</u> we "run the race", "fight the good fight" and "hang in there all the way" as Brother Paul said & did, our reward is great indeed! But, even more, to me personally, I'm a man who has <u>always</u> "paid his debts".

Before I accepted Christ Jesus on 3/11/97, even though I hadn't killed anyone in (30) years now, I used to give "Tit for Tat". You hurt me, I hurt you back- only (10) times as bad if I could. I'm no longer "proud" of this. In fact, I am now ashamed of it. Even so, it is the truth. But, even worse, even though I now profess Christ Jesus as my Lord & Savior, "old habits" are hard to break. Racial hatreds run deep within me and are very hard to break- or forgive. But, as always, with Christ Jesus in my heart & soul, I shall overcome and claim the victory in His name. Whenever I do my will and not His, when I "stray" away from Him, in time, usually within a week or two, He "convicts" me and I feel so miserable, I feel so "vile & filthy" so "unclean" that my own soul gives off a putrid, rotting, vile smell that won't go away! Praise God for that! Because of His love for <u>me</u>, He "convicts" me and I finally hit the cell floor on my knees and "get right" with God. It is shameful, painful, and humiliating. I literally cry & sob and "snot" runs down my nose and all over my lips & chin! Truth! But Praise God for it! Because, when I hit my knees & pray long & hard, when I really & truly repent & beg for forgiveness and to be "clean" again, He does exactly that! Thank You Jesus! Even more, He infuses my heart & soul with a thirst to serve Him in <u>all</u> areas of my life. It is easy to accept Christ Jesus as "Savior". We all want to be "saved" from "spiritual death" and/or "Hell" and feel safe & secure in the majestic presence of God Himself. But we rebel about the "Lord" part. It's stupid & foolish because it's futile to "rebel" against God! But we do. We just want to have "fun" which is usually a euphemism for "sin". (Drugs, Sex, Drinking, Fighting, Cursing, Gambling, Etc.) And when we do these things, knowing they are wrong & sinful, we are in a state of "rebellion" or "direct & knowing disobedience" to God. But, as always, He will bring us out of it after we get "soured" & " stinking" & totally miserable. So bottom line? I "owe" my Lord & Savior Christ Jesus an enormous "debt" that <u>I</u> <u>know</u> I can't "repay" or "make right". Even so, because of my propensity for <u>always</u> paying my debts, I've <u>got</u> to make every effort I can to make "his load lighter" and become "lock, stock, & barrel" a willing "slave" to Christ Jesus! Praise His Holy, Holy Name! Now & Forever- Glory & Praise to Him!! He "stood up" for <u>me</u>. He "paid the price" I can't really comprehend for <u>me</u>! He, as we say in prison, "went my bail" when <u>no</u> <u>one</u> <u>else</u> <u>would</u>! How can I not at least try to repay Him at least a tiny, tiny, tiny, miniscule part of what He paid for me?

LeAnn, we can't call on "phone cards". We can't even save our family & friends money by calling the so-called "bargain numbers" like "***-***-***" or any other. On your card, I can call your number, ***-***-****, but only <u>collect</u>. One (15) minute phone call runs about $4.50 to $6.50. I want very much to talk with you. Even to pray with you even more! (Smile!) But, in (3) years, I've never once asked you for anything but your friendship, your love & your continued service to God! You are my friend and my child/baby sister and my sister in Christ. I will not "use you" in any way. If you want me to call you at your home phone or a friend's phone, you tell me a day, time & date and I'll do so. Example? Gladly! (Smile!) (Roger, 11-6-99, at 8:00 P.M. your time, 11:00 P.M. my time, call me at ***-***-**** or ***-***-**** or whatever number you give me! Bye!!) (Smile!) Hope we can do it.

No, there isn't anything you could send me except more <u>regular</u> <u>letters</u>, as you used to do, (Shame on you! Smile!) and perhaps a few more pictures like this small graduation picture. Blow it up! (8x10) Also I'd like some of you in the "Dixie Flag", Prom Night dress you promised but haven't yet done. And, <u>if</u> <u>possible</u>, a concrete date, time & number for (1) (15) minute call. <u>That</u>, my young female friend, would indeed make an excellent Christmas gift. <u>Not </u>money. Not cigarettes. Not even Chocolate Fudge with pecans. Just a simple phone call! (Please?) (Smile!)

LeAnn "Featherwood" Redding, I truly love you in a deep, pure way. I do! You're a "joy" in my life. I enjoyed your problems & your successes. Most of all I enjoyed what makes "you"- "you"!! (Smile!) And Christ Jesus loves <u>you</u> girl!! <u>Very</u> <u>Much</u>!!

Jesus Loves You & so do I,

-Roger Dale-

P.S.

Seven (7) hours to write this "book." Hope you enjoy it. Hope you receive my message. Serve Jesus! Always.

Love You, "F" 10/27/99

10-26-99

Le Ann,

Hello "Featherwood"! Or maybe you have become a young woman and no longer like that name(?) It happens. Most so-called "nicknames" are loved and cherished by young kids but they become "boring" to older people. However, as I told you before, in prison, which is all I truly know, for a "good wood", ("Peckerwood") usually a young white Southern boy, being called a "Peckerwood" or "Good Wood" is considered a big "honor" or compliment. And, as with all other things, quite naturally, these type of people, like me, pass the "honor" or compliment along when we run across a "good" white girl. We call them "Featherwood". Be that as it may, both you & I have a higher calling; we both are believers in, and followers of, Christ Jesus! Praise His Most Holy Name! Glory!!

I've now known you for (3) years and I truly cherish your friendship. Your very simply a beautiful person; inside and out. Your beauty is in your smile & in your heart. You absolutely "radiate" love, compassion & understanding. That is very rare at any age — but especially rare in one so young. It is very simply a

(OVER)

pleasure to know you. Jo Ann, your mom and dad did an excellent job of raising you. It is easy to see that they instilled in you a sense of morality and compassion. Even if you, at (15) years old, did want to contact Charlie and get a letter from him, you had no way of knowing just how your # 1 "contact" with people like Charlie & I might turn out. Nor did you have any way of knowing that Charlie was illiterate and can barely read or write. Nor did you have any idea that a native Tennesseean, me, would be the first one to respond to your letter. Nor could either of us know that we would both be "Homies" living in Lexington, Tennessee! (Smile)

But, your "first contact" (Smile) letter was very, very well crafted and extremely well written by a (15) years old kid!! There simply was no choice for me. I had to respond and, in time, after I had set certain conditions, Charlie, too, has come to like you a lot. I have come to love you a whole lot. You, my young friend, are like my own child, which I've never had, and my younger sisters, which I do have!! Though all of them are now in their (30's)! Even more importantly, you are, like me, a "true" "child of God". Though all humans are God's "children", only the ones whom make a deliberate decision or "choice" to to acknowledge him as both our "Father" and our "God" / "Lord" are His "true children". It is our "choice" to make and both of us have sincerely & truly made our choice — and — because of this one decision, the most important "decision" or "choice" any human being can ever make, we share a "bond" ("Followers of Christ") ("Christians") that can <u>never</u> be broken". We, my beautiful young sister will soon be spending an "eternity" with our Lord & Savior Christ Jesus". And though we don't truly comprehend or appreciate just how long an "eternity" is, we human beings having a so-called "finite" mind, once we are called "home" (Heaven), we will in addition to our "glorified bodies" have an "infinite" mind and will then ~~know~~ what an "eternity" in the presence of our "Heavenly Father's" love, mercy & grace truly means". Glory to God Almighty & thank you Jesus"! When we are young, we often think we are "invulnerable" and "impervious" to "Death". It truly very seldom enters our minds, as individuals or collectively in a group, that we might "die". "Death" is something which happens to "old people" or maybe "sick people" but not to young, healthy kids entering into the prime of our life". Then, on "~~Prom~~ Night" or maybe just (4) or (5) of us "hanging-out" with our so-

(OVER) called "friends" — well — maybe we drink

a few beers too many. Maybe we even sip a taste of "shine" or maybe we do a couple of "joints" or "doobies". Maybe even a combination of all three. I mean, hey', we are young and we are just trying to have a little "fun". Man, Lexington is just a little "hick town" and other than Friday night football games, in season, there simply isn't a whole lot to do'! We just want to have a little "fun"! That's all. But, on that very night, some man puts away a few too many at the local pub and, "accidently", even though we are smart and use the "designated driver" (usually the more responsible/mature friend amongst us) well, old "Bubba" doesn't give a hoot about all that "kid stuff". And a few days later, "Bubba" and all of us "friends" are laid to rest. Tragic? Yes, definitely! But, LeAnn "Featherwood" Redding, you are the "luckiest" one of all of us "friends". You knew Christ Jesus'! You accepted Him early on in your life and you will indeed have a new & glorious life, a life without end and without any sickness and death'. You will, for all eternity, bask in the love & glory that only our Lord is able & ready to give to every single one of us that made the "decision/choice" to accept Him completely & with absolutely no reservations as both "Savior" and "Lord"'! Glory girl'! Glory! But, maybe our other (4) "friends" didn't make that

(5.) "choice/decision" and no such "life" is in store for them. Maybe our Lord, in His infinite mercy, love & grace for each one of us poor human beings in our ignorance & defiance, regardless of age, color or sexual gender, will display his compassion and those whom didn't make that one simple choice/decision will be granted that one so-called "second death" and simply cease to exist after "Judgement Day". We simply don't know what God will do. And, most Holy Father, maybe their futures will be so terrible & horrible in the "Pit" that it puts cold "goose bumps" all over my body! After all, we are told unequivocably that one poor soul in "Hell" begged God for just one single drop of water to lick off the rotted flesh on the finger of a "Leper". And God said simply: "No". And, when the former "rich man" that walked past that wasted, wretched, rotted "Leper" each day and never once stopped to give any assistance and/or help in any way, shape, fashion or form, saw that God was not moved by his begging, the poor man told God, "Well, Lord, I've got (5) brothers still living and none are "saved". Please, Lord, please let me tell them what has happened to me and cause them not to come where I am! Or, if that isn't even possible, will you, Lord, please see that they get my message?" And, our Lord said, "They, like you, have ears that

6.

will not hear and eyes that will not see." In all of God's Holy Word ("Holy Bible"), other than the things Christ Jesus bore for us, that one story is, to me, simply a "hideous" existence! There is no "life", no "love", no "mercy", no "grace", no "compassion" from our Lord. Even so, since He is "infallible" and cannot make a "mistake" or render an "unjust judgement", we, as "true children" of God, must accept the absolute reality of what took place with this poor wretched soul. He had a million, million opportunities to make his "choice / decision" but he chose not to accept Christ Jesus as Lord & Savior! Was he "stupid"? Well, despite the money and "social class" from whence he came, giving him the very best education & training possible, he deliberately chose to reject Christ Jesus (the Son) and God (the Father) and the Holy Spirit. So, yes indeed he was, and forever more will be, "stupid". But, given where he was then, is now, and will be forever more, being "stupid" is the very least of his troubles! No, his condition does not "please" me nor do I take any pleasure whatsoever in where he is at and in what horrible, hideous condition he will spend all eternity! Nor do I take this story "lightly". Just the reverse. I take it very seriously indeed. In fact, to be absolutely truthful and entirely candid with you, Je Ann, I am terrified, scared witless by this story."

You see, these other (5) souls were his "brothers" not simply his "friends", and they, too, would end up where he was, and all (6) of them, still are this very day — and will be forever + ever, "time without end" — for all "eternity"!! As hideous as this knowledge is, and it is indeed the most horrible story I've read in the "Word" of God, excepting the "hideousness" that Jesus endured for us, it shows a personal side of God that none of us are "comfortable" with. Oh yes! we are all "comfortable" with all of the "stories" of God's love, grace, mercy and compassion. They calm us and give us a feeling of "safety" + "secureness". And why is this? Because, we made our "choice / decision" to accept, surrender + obey Christ Jesus!! And, because of this choice / decision we, you + I, made, we are "saved" from having to ever personally see this "side" of our God! And thank God for it!! You see, God truly is at "war" with "the enemy" (Satan) and though Christ Jesus has already won the victory and "saved" us if we "choose" Him over (satan) and defeated "Death" + "sin", God, for reasons we don't know now, but will know when He calls us "Home", still allows (satan) "the enemy" the time God promised him. But, Je Ann, we, you + I, don't have to "sweat it". We are, by the very blood + death of Christ Jesus, "healed" and "saved". Period! Praise Him girl!

(OVER)

But, LeAnn, those "friends" of ours? and, yes, even the people we "dislike" (like poor old "Bubba") we must give "witness" to at each & every opportunity we have. This is not only our "duty" to Christ Jesus, it is also a direct order from God! There is nothing to "argue" about. No, being human, there are times we simply don't "feel like it". That is true. But, LeAnn, there is no doubt that Christ Jesus didn't "feel like" going through what He endured for us, all of us, every single one of us! In fact, He spent the entire night in that garden praying to His "true father" and asking that, if possible, "this cup be allowed to pass from me". But, in the end, because of His enormous love and respect for his one "true father", the same Father that He had spent time without measure with through all the aeons, eons & aeons of time with prior to his birth in human form, He simply bowed His majestic head and quietly said, "Thy Will Be Done". Total and absolute obedience to His Father and to our Father through Christ Jesus! Glory!!

LeAnn, do you know what absolutely impressed me the most about Christ Jesus during His (33) years in the body of a man? Surprisingly it wasn't the "miracles" He performed. It wasn't the pain & humiliation He endured just before & during His execution in a most heinous manner even though that was bad enough to make me "wince" - and cry!!

When He begged for a single drink of water in His pain & misery on that Cross, some very sick & perverted "demon" in the guise of a Roman soldier had the absolute cruelty & visciousness to put a sponge full of "vinegar" — not water — on the end of his spear and press it to His bloodied & cracked lips to drink!! It was not even this cowardly & demonic act that gets me. But, again, I've cried about this one single, sadistic act many times. If you think about it, you will too!

Le Ann, Jesus never knew "sin". Never! God "hates", not "dislikes", "hates" sin so much that He cannot bear to see it. Think about it! God turns His face from "sin"!! Big or little "sins", to God, "sin is sin" and He simply cannot tolerate it — period!! Can you imagine a newborn baby, in perfect health & perfect in body, mind & soul? The newborn is human and feels all that we feel. Fresh from the womb of a good mother where there was nothing "bad" to him/her as a fetus. No drugs, no alchohol, no tobacco products, no smog, no "bad" things period. Conceived in love, carried (9) months in a "clean womb" with no disease and delivered quickly with no troubles, complications or discomfort. This newborn, innocent child is placed on a large round table made of solid cold metal with no "padding" or cloth of any kind. He/she starts to whimper in discomfort and gets very cold from the very cold

(OVER)

steel table very fast. Around this very large round cold steel table are numerous sick, psychotic, truly evil people with some very, very cold steel pliars, knives, scapels, forks and numerous other instruments of torture & pain causing capability. And others have hot coals, blowtorches, molten lava, etc (you get the idea.) They all start working, systematically, to deliver the utmost pain & injuries to this totally innocent newborn which has never once known pain & discomfort —. but none-the-less feels every single (grunnion?) of the pain and screams & screams in pure and completely unadulterated pain & terror! Turns your stomach? Well it should. Mine too! But this is simply an "illustration" as bad as it sounds and the sickness it conveys is only "illusionary". It never happened although the "Nazis" came close to it in W.W. II at several of their "camps".

But, Je Ann, Jesus had never known "sin" period! And, like His Holy Father, He simply couldn't tolerate it in any manner—Period! (Not even a "little white lie" ("FIB"), stealing, rape or murder nor even "worship of satan.") "Sin" is "Sin" — And before Christ Jesus — "the wages of "sin" are death." Period! And since every single human being but Christ Jesus that has ever lived, from "Adam & Eve" all the way up to 1999 with "Adam & Steve" has "sinned" thousands, if not millions of times,

(11.)

during our respective life times, before Christ Jesus, there simply wasn't any "attonement" for what we all did and did very well indeed! It was and has always been within our very nature to "sin" — and in so doing — to incur the "Wrath of God" and suffer the death that our sins brought upon each and every single one of us". Every single human being but Christ Jesus. In Him — there was no "sin" — Period!

But, Je Ann, at the very worst time in his short life in a human body (33 years), beaten, whipped, scourged, spat upon, humiliated & finally nailed to a Cross, when He was at his weakest point in body, mind & spirit, crucified on that cross (Cross), He bore the "sins of the entire world"! Glory! Thank You Sweet Jesus!

Think of it! He whom had never known sin, could not in fact bear to see sin in any manner, shape or form — every single sin ever committed before His glorious birth in human form, during His short but all so glorious life span of only (33) years, and every single sin committed over the past nearly 2,000 years and every single sin still to be committed until humanity as we know it comes to an end, was borne by that totally "newborn" on an old wooden, rugged cross instead of a large round cold steel table! And Je Ann, Jesus also cried out in unspeakable & terribly hideous pain & terror — and even

(OVER)

(12)

though He had been with God the Father for uncountable billions & trillions of years, time uncountable, aeons, eons & oceans of time, and was
"One with the Father" during all that time, He
literally was so overwhelmed with that load of "sin",
our sin, yours & mine, as well as every sin
ever committed by every single human being who ever
lived, is living now, and ever will live until
"Judgement Day" when all humanity ceases
to exist in the form we are now in. He
got every sin ever committed laid on His body,
mind & soul! And His absolute terror & agony
was so great He screamed, "My God,
hast thou forsaken me?" He didn't
make a statement. He was in doubt. He
asked a question! Have you any concept
of the magnitude of his agony & terror &
absolute, total helplessness that would
make Him question whether or not His
One & Only True Father would totally
leave Him alone in his human and
His "Godly" suffering? It is absolutely
inconceivable for Christ Jesus to
question the one & only God" with
Which He is "One With"? Then
He "died" a human death. And, most
glorious of all things, (3) days later
He was Resurrected by God the Father
and "Sin" & "Death" were totally defeated for all time! Glory to the Father!
Glory to the Son! Glory to the Holy
Spirit! Glory! "3 in 1" = GOD!!

(13.)

Now, that impresses me! That stirs my blood! That, to me, is the true definition of exactly what "God the Father" meant when it was written in His Word, "For God so loved the world —————". (John 3:16) Is it any wonder I want to witness? Is it any wonder that I want to carry the "gospel" ("good news") to anyone whom will listen? No, I simply am not capable of "repaying" my Lord & Savior Christ Jesus for that (what He suffered when that whole load of "sin" came down on Him). And I can't "earn" my way into "Glory" because it can't be done. But, LeAnn, "Featherwood", I can not tell a lie I usually tell. I can not think an evil thought I used to love. I can not do an "abomination" with some young & foolish "girly boy" whom I used to dearly love. In short, I can lessen that "load of sin" that my Glorious Lord & Savior Christ Jesus bore on that dark day by not doing even (1) stinking so-called "little sin" or "major sin" even though, to God, "sin is sin" - Period! And every "sin" I don't do lessens that load He carried that dark but glorious day! Thank You Lord Jesus! And every "sin" you don't do, does the same thing! And every "sin" that someone else doesn't do because we bore witness to them and revealed what God revealed to us, also lightens that awful load even more. We you & I, can make a difference. We

(14) both _can_ make a difference. We both can tell everyone we meet the "Good News", the absolutely wonderful news of the "Gospel of Jesus Christ". We _can_ spread His love + mercy and grace! We _can_, as both God the Father + Christ Jesus the Son, ~~commands~~ us to do, not "asks" or "requests" us to do, but "orders" us to do, Love one another and surrender our hearts, bodies + souls, to Christ Jesus and do His Will — not our own wills! And, if we "run the race", "fight the good fight" and "hang in there all the way" as Brother Paul said + did, our reward is great indeed! But, even more, to me personally, I'm a man whom has _always_ "paid his debts". ~~Before~~ Before I accepted Christ Jesus on 3/11/97, even though I hadn't ~~killed~~ killed anyone in (30) years now, I used to give "Tit for Tat". You hurt me, I hurt you back + only (10) times as bad if I could. I'm no longer "proud" of this. In fact, I am now ashamed of it. Even so, it is the truth. But, even worse, even though I now profess Christ Jesus as my Lord + Savior, "old habits" are hard to break. Racial hatreds run deep within me and are very hard to break — or forgive. ██████████████████. But, as always, with Christ Jesus in my heart + soul, I shall overcome and claim the victory in His name. Whenever I do my will and not His, when I "stray" away from Him,

(15.) in time, usually within a week or two, He "convicts" me and I feel so miserable, I feel so "vile & filthy," so "unclean" that my own soul gives off a "putrid, rotting, vile smell" that won't go away! Praise God for that! Because of His love for me, He "convicts" me and I finally hit the cell floor on my knees and "get right" with God. It is shameful, painful and humiliating. I literally cry & sob and "snot" runs down my nose and all over my lips & chin! Truth! But, Praise God for it! Because, when I hit my knees & pray long & hard, when I really & truly repent & beg for forgiveness and to be "clean" again, He does exactly that! Thank You Jesus! Even more, He infuses my heart & soul with a thirst to serve Him in all areas of my life. It is easy to accept Christ Jesus as "Savior". We all want to be "saved" from "spiritual death" and/or "Hell" and feel safe & secure in the majestic presence of God Himself. But, we rebel about the "Lord" part. It's stupid & foolish because it's futile to "rebel" against God! But, we do. We just want to have "fun" which is usually a euphemism for "sin". (Drugs, Sex) Drinking, Fighting, Cursing, Gambling, etc.) And when we do these things, knowing they are wrong & sinful, we are in a state of "rebellion" or "direct & knowing disobedience" to God. But, as always, He will bring us out of it

(OVER) after we get "soured" & "stinking" & totally miserable.

16.

So, bottom line? I "owe" my Lord & Savior Christ Jesus an enormous "debt" that I know I can't "repay" or "make right". Even so, because of my propensity for always paying my debts, I've got to make every effort I can to make "his load lighter" and become "lock, stock & barrell" a "willing "slave" to Christ Jesus! Praise His Holy, Holy Name! Now & Forever — Glory & Praise to Him!! He "stood up" for me. He "paid the price" I can't really comprehend for me! He, as we say in prison, "went my bail" when no one else would! How can I not at least try to repay him at least a tiny, tiny, tiny, miniscule part of what He paid for me?

Je Ann, we can't call on "phone cards". We can't even save our family & friends money by calling the so-called "bargain numbers" like ██-██-██ or any other. On your card, I can call your number, ██-██-██, but only collect. One (15) minute phone call runs about $4.50 to $6.50. I want very much to talk with you. Even to pray with you even more! (Smile!) But! in (3) years, I've never once asked you for anything but your friendship, your love & your continued service to God! You are my friend and my child/baby sister and my sister in Christ. I will not "use you"

(17)

in any way. If you want me to call you at your home phone or a friend's phone, you tell me a day, time & date and I'll do so. Example? Gladly! (Smile!) (Roger, 11-6-99, at 8:00P.M. your time, 11:00P.M. my time, call me at ██-██-██ or ██-██-██ or whatever number you give me! Bye!) (Smile!) Hope we can do it.

No, there isn't anything you could send me except more regular letters, as you used to do, (Shame on you! Smile!) and perhaps a few more pictures like this small graduation picture. Blow it up! (8×10) Also I'd like one of you in the "Dixie Flag" Prom Night dress you promised but haven't yet done. And, if possible, a concrete date, time & number for (1) (15) minute call. That, my young female friend, would indeed make an Excellent Christmas gift. Not money. Not cigarettes. Not even Chocolate Fudge with pecans. Just a simple phone call! (Please?) (Smile!)

"Le Ann" "Heatherwood" "Redding, I truly love you in a deep, pure way. I do! Your a "Joy" in my life. I enjoyed your problems & your successes. Most of all I enjoyed what makes "you" — "you"!! (Smile!) And Christ Jesus loves you girl!! Very Much!!

Jesus Loves You & so do I,
— Roger Dale —

P.S. Seven (7) hours to write this "book." Hope you enjoy it. Hope you receive my message. Some day! Always. Love You "F" 10/27/99

As far as the East is from the West, so far hath He removed our transgressions from us.

(Psalm 103:12 KJV)

Since no man is excluded from calling upon God, the gate of salvation is open to all. There is nothing else to hinder us from entering but our own disbelief.

(John Calvin)

CLOSURE

I have always believed our Lord puts people into our lives for a reason—the right person at the right time. Roger Dale was my person. He was the friend I needed when no other friend would do. He listened carefully and patiently through all my teenage drama and understood what it was like to grow up feeling different.

But no matter how contrasting our lives turned out to be, we had one common thread that always held us close: our love for Jesus. Roger Dale found his way back through death and sin and into the open, loving arms of the Savior.

James 4:7 (NIV) says, "Submit yourselves then to God, resist the devil and he will flee from you."

Roger Dale submitted, giving his life back to the only One who could ever save him from his life of wickedness and to the only One who could ever bring him back into the glory of God. He submitted to Jesus and accepted His love and full forgiveness.

Full forgiveness? For a murderer? Yes. Roger Dale was covered by the blood of Jesus's sacrifice on the cross. All his sins were now gone, washed away. He was made new in the eyes of God! He *knew* that even someone like him, someone who had committed such atrocities and deceit, could be forgiven by accepting Jesus as his Savior. He *knew* that even someone like him was loved by God—loved so much that He sent His only Son to pay the ultimate price on the cross. He *knew* that even someone like him could go to heaven and spend eternity with our Lord Jesus.

My dear friend did just that. In February 2004, Roger Dale lost his battle with cancer. While his death still saddens me and I feel a hole where his friendship was, I am happy to know my friend is exactly where he wanted to be: in heaven with Jesus! He knew he would be greeted with open arms and a smile as a beloved son returning home!

And I know I will see him one day, arms stretched wide, finally able to give me that long-awaited hug!

RESOURCES

NIV Women's Devotional Bible, Grand Rapids, Michigan: Zondervan Bible Publishing, 2012.

Anderson, Ken, *Where to Find It in the Bible: The Ultimate A to Z Resource.* Nashville: Thomas Nelson Publishers, 1996.

52 Bible Verses You Should Have on Your Heart, Nashville: B&H Publishing Group 2016.

Stanley, Charles, In Touch Ministries, https://www.intouch.org.

Graham, Billy, Billy Graham Evangelistic Association, https://billygraham.org.

Meyer, Joyce, Joyce Meyer Ministries, https://joycemeyer.org

Our Daily Bread, https://ourdailybread.org.

All about God, https://www.allaboutgod.com

Wikipedia, https://www.wikipedia.org/.

Brainy Quote, https://www.brainyquote.com/.

Merriam-Webster, https://www.merriam-webster.com.

Printed in the United States
by Baker & Taylor Publisher Services